T0317816

AMAZING CHICKEN RECIPES FROM CHEF MATT HORN'S RESTAURANT AND HOME KITCHEN

MATT HORN

HARVARD
COMMON
PRESS

Quarto.com

© 2024 Quarto Publishing Group USA Inc.
Text © 2024 Matt Horn
Photography © 2024 Andrew Thomas Lee, except as noted below

First Published in 2024 by The Harvard Common Press, an imprint of The Quarto Group,
100 Cummings Center, Suite 265-D, Beverly, MA 01915, USA.
T (978) 282-9590 F (978) 283-2742

The Harvard Common Press titles are also available at discount for retail, wholesale,
promotional, and bulk purchase. For details, contact the Special Sales Manager by email
at specialsales@quarto.com or by mail at The Quarto Group, Attn: Special Sales Manager,
100 Cummings Center, Suite 265-D, Beverly, MA 01915, USA.

28 27 26 25 24   1 2 3 4 5

ISBN: 978-0-7603-8741-2

Digital edition published in 2024
eISBN: 978-0-7603-8742-9

Library of Congress Cataloging-in-Publication Data is available.

Design: Cindy Samargia Laun
Photography: pages 7, 8 (left), 9 (left), 34, 37, 40-131, 134-145 by Andrew Thomas Lee;
pages 18, 19, 27, 33, 38, 162, 170 courtesy of Matt Horn; pages 1-6, 8 (right), 9 (right), 10,
17, 28, 132, 150, 152, 160, 164, 169 by Shutterstock

Printed in China

Dedication

This book is a heartfelt homage to the multitude of souls and stories that paved my culinary journey. My radiant mother, Enola Brown, is at the forefront, whose daily display of unwavering faith, manifested in her beautiful smile, is my guiding light. Mommy, your belief in me is both my strength and sanctuary; your love is a force that propels me, even when the path is strewn with challenges. To my hearts, Nina, Matthew, and Leilani, you aren't just the beacon lights of my life but the perpetual fire and joy in my soul; even eternity feels too short to celebrate our bond. Each Kowbird guest breathed life into this journey, turning every dish from mere food to memories and acting as the wind beneath my wings, powering the heart of each creation. My ancestors, ever present in spirit, have carved traditions into my very being, connecting me with the land and tales of old. And then there's Oakland, this vivacious community that doesn't merely dine but delves deep into the stories and legacies served on the plate. Every page of this book intertwines tribute, gratitude, and boundless love and is an earnest dedication to all who are part of this soulful expedition. Power to the people.

Contents

**WHY DID THE CHICKEN
CROSS THE ROAD? 21**

**THE SOUTHERN ROOTS
OF KOWBIRD:
CHICKEN, CULTURE,
AND COMMUNITY 31**

5

6

DESSERTS 115

SOUTHERN SAUCES 133

7

GRAVIES FOR CHICKEN 141

8

SEASONINGS FOR CHICKEN 153

Foreword

By Lolis Eric Elie

"A Chicken Ain't Nothing But a Bird," Emmett "Babe" Wallace declared way back in 1940, and musical luminaries like Cab Calloway and Louis Jordan put his tune on wax and spread the message.

Of course they were wrong.

To say "a chicken ain't nothing but a bird" is to try to cut this common delicacy down to size. It is to say that any declaration you may have heard to the contrary, at its base a chicken is a fowl much like any other. But what other fowl has traveled so widely, found a home in such a wide array of pots and pits, or adapted itself to the seasonings and predilections of such an expanse of countries, ethnicities, races, and classes? Measured by that standard, the chicken sits alone on a lofty perch. No other bird comes close.

The chicken is the "gospel bird," served as secular sacrament after Sunday service. But it is also the "yard bird," of Charlie "Yardbird" Parker fame—an animal so common that it could be found in damn near any yard in rural America and many yards in lots of other places. It is the coq au vin, steeped in Burgundy wine, but it is also the protein of choice at gas stations and dives everywhere.

Fried chicken and barbecue are culinary signatures of the Black American South. And, though their addresses are in Oakland, California, Matt Horn's restaurants, Kowbird and Horn Barbecue, have their roots in the kitchens of Southern grandmothers. So it is fitting that, having mastered the alchemy of turning meat and smoke into barbecue of the highest order, Matt Horn would turn his attention to celebrating the chicken.

Matt does in this book what he did so well in *Horn Barbecue*, his debut publication. He treats the reader like a very smart student. He goes over the basics slowly enough so as to educate the uninitiated, but not so slowly as to bore the more experienced reader. He also provides details and insights that he has gained from hours spent practicing his craft. Between these covers, he takes us through many of the chicken's culinary permutations—fried, *jambalayed*, Bourbon-glazed, and *dumpling'ed*. In clear prose, he has made these recipes easy to follow yet full of soul and flavor.

When I arrived at Horn Barbecue one sunny Oakland Sunday, there was a line down the block. That's how big a reputation this man's food had earned.

I'm confident that if you follow these recipes, you'll have folks lined up, if not down the block, then at least at the stove begging for seconds.

Lolis Eric Elie, a writer, journalist, television producer, documentary filmmaker, and food historian, is the author of *Smokestack Lightning: Adventures in the Heart of Barbecue Country* and *Treme: Stories and Recipes from the Heart of New Orleans*.

INTRODUCTION

—

From Hen to Table

The traditions—agricultural, culinary, familial, and cultural—that inform my cooking, at Kowbird and my other restaurants, and at home, originate primarily from one place: the South. While the South is celebrated for many signature foods—from collards, okra, and mustard greens to pork shoulder, beef brisket, and all kinds of ribs—I've come to believe that the unheralded heart of Southern cooking is, quite simply, chicken. Relatively easy to grow in one's own backyard or a small plot of land, relatively inexpensive to buy from a neighboring farmer or the grocery store, chicken is core food, the main-dish protein, that has sustained many generations of Southerners, right up to the present. This book is an homage to that tradition and a celebration of its stories and its flavors.

In the soulful stretches of the American South, the gentle murmurs of ancestral tales waft through the air on the tantalizing aromas of age-old recipes simmering on stovetops. When one mentions Southern cuisine, the mind's eye conjures visions of family tables laden with an array of dishes, each telling its own story of the lands, trials, and triumphs seen before. The humble chicken is at the heart of these stories, standing resilient and evocative. It's not just an ingredient; it's a chronicle, a vessel for memories, and the very essence of the South's rich cultural tapestry.

The landscape of the South is vast and varied, from the sun-drenched plains of Texas to the rolling hills of Tennessee and the lush swamplands of Louisiana. While this land has seen its share of historical upheavals, its peoples' profound connection to the earth remains unwavering. The soil, after all, not only nurtures crops but also cradles the legacies of generations past. And in that soil, amid fields of golden corn and green beans, scurries our hero—the chicken.

Each cluck and flutter echo the rhythm of Southern blues, jazz, and gospel. In its call, we hear the songs of Bessie Smith, the prose of Faulkner, and the speeches of King. Chicken isn't merely sustenance; it's a symphony. When we tuck into Southern Fried Chicken (page 43) or Chicken Gumbo with Andouille Sausage (page 63), we're not just tasting flavors but imbibing histories. These dishes bear the imprints of African, European, and Indigenous American influences, a testament to the South's diverse heritage. As this bird moves from the coop to our table, it brings a grandmother's infused love, fathers barbecuing under the summer sky, and children savoring their first bite of golden, crispy drumsticks.

The South is an intricate dance of traditions, some passed down through written recipes and others through whispers from one generation to the next. It's a land where food is not just consumed but revered. Every bite tells of bountiful harvests and lean periods, love found and lost, and dreams realized and shattered. This connection to the past is palpable in every Southern kitchen, where pots and pans carry a legacy.

It's easy to overlook chicken amid the dazzling array of Southern dishes. Still, you must remember: This bird witnessed the region's ever-evolving history, trials and triumphs, and enduring spirit. Whether grilled on a summer evening, stewed on a chilly winter day, or fried to golden perfection for a family gathering, chicken is a canvas painted with the rich hues of the South's diverse palette.

As we journey from hen to table, we're not just exploring recipes but traveling through time. On each page, recipes are an invitation to partake in a story simmering for centuries and seasoned with tears, laughter, love, and resilience; to understand that behind every meal is a multitude of hands—those that sowed the land, nurtured the flock, and lovingly crafted each dish; to recognize when you savor a piece of chicken, you're not just indulging in a meal but participating in a tradition as old as the South itself.

As we embark on this flavorful journey, we must pay honor to each recipe and understand that the essence captured on these pages is not merely culinary but profoundly spiritual. It's a celebration of a land that has always found solace, unity, and identity in its food despite its tumultuous past. *Kowbird* is more than a cookbook; it's a tribute, a love letter to the South and its indomitable spirit.

So, as you turn the pages, hear the sizzle, smell the aromas, and, most important, feel the love and legacy embedded in each recipe. Let's celebrate the South with its soul-defining stories, landscapes, and culinary traditions and the foods that the South has shared with the rest of the world, including here in California, where I cook and write. Let's honor the chicken, too, not as an ingredient but as an emblem of the South's enduring heartbeat.

Your journey through the heart of Southern cuisine begins now.

1

WHY DID THE CHICKEN CROSS THE ROAD?

The answer to that age-old question might remain a mystery, but the chicken's journey through the culinary landscape is profound and enduring.

From rustic farmyards to the opulent tables of upscale dining establishments, this bird's story is imbued with layers, memories, and culture.

Chicken held a special place in our lives as we grew up, adapting and transforming according to seasons, occasions, or moods. The comforting presence of frozen potpies on cold evenings or the simple childhood joy of McDonald's nuggets speaks to chicken's versatility.

And memories often intertwine with traditions—recipes shared from one generation to the next. These dishes are more than just meals; they carry stories echoing the trials and triumphs of past generations, spanning geographies.

Chicken can transport us back in time. Remember the aroma of your grandmother's chicken stew simmering slowly on the stovetop, promising warmth and love? Or that time during college when you tried an ambitious chicken recipe for your roommates, marking your first foray into the vast world of culinary arts?

Chicken's versatility is also evident as it dances gracefully through global cuisines—from aromatic Indian curries to the char-grilled skewers of Japanese yakitori, the flavorful French coq au vin and the zestful delight that is Mexican tinga.

In many cultures, chicken is connected to rites of passage. In some places, a chicken dish is prepared to celebrate a child's birth; in others, it signifies abundance and prosperity as part of a wedding feast. It is a dish we prepare to impress someone special as well as a comfort food we lean on during tough times.

Chicken remains an emblem of home, warmth, and shared memories. It offers a familiar embrace, whether as Sunday dinner, picnic fare, or late-night comfort food.

In the Southern United States, the chicken's role is particularly significant. The bird becomes a cultural icon, a symbol of history, resilience, and community, offering flavors, lessons, and memories deeply entrenched in the region's ethos. The simple chicken is also emblematic of perseverance and transformation. Although its origins may be humble, the bird's rise to culinary stardom is a testament to its universal appeal and adaptability.

As time progressed, chicken became a more complex and nuanced ingredient. It was no longer just about comfort; it became about exploration and innovation. Culinary enthusiasts and chefs experimented, infusing chicken with contemporary twists, introducing exotic ingredients, and presenting it in previously unimagined ways. From molecular gastronomy that deconstructs the chicken to its very essence to fusion dishes that blend traditions, chicken is ready to play its part. Despite this culinary experimentation, its essence remains unchanged—the bird that warms our hearts, satiates our hunger, and stokes our memories.

Perhaps what's most profound is the chicken's ability to unite. In a world brimming with differences, the love for chicken is a universal thread. It's a silent reminder that simple joys and flavors bind us all, regardless of where we come from or where we're headed.

In the grand tapestry of life, where challenges and crossroads abound, the story of the chicken is a comforting constant, reminding us of the beauty of shared tales and the magic of simple, unadulterated flavors. Although we may never uncover the mystery of its road-crossing endeavors, we can take solace in the rich, flavorful journey it offers us daily.

Chicken Breeds

Chickens are incredibly diverse, with about 1,600 breeds and varieties recognized by poultry associations worldwide. Here's a list of some of the more popular and distinct chicken breeds:

LARGE FOWL BREEDS

Australorp	Developed in Australia from Black Orpingtons, this breed has glossy black feathers with a green sheen, and a large red comb. These chickens are renowned for their record-breaking egg-laying capabilities, sometimes blue or bluish eggs, and calm demeanor.
Brahma	Notable for their enormous size and feathered legs and toes, Brahmas are the calm and gentle giants of the chicken world. They're winter-hardy and are kept for meat and eggs.
Cochin	Recognized for their soft, fluffy appearance and feathered legs and toes, Cochins are kept more for ornamental reasons than for egg production. Their gentle, friendly nature makes them a favorite for those seeking pet chickens.
Leghorn	A highly active and hardy breed, Leghorns are prolific layers, with the white variety being the most recognizable. They're known for their slender build and upright tails.
Orpington	Originating from Great Britain, Orpingtons, often called Buff Orpingtons, are large, fluffy birds known for their gentle temperament. They come in various colors and are appreciated for their meat and substantial egg production.
Plymouth Rock (Barred Rock)	This breed, known for its characteristic black-and-white striped feathers, is a versatile bird often kept for its meat and egg-laying abilities. Its docile nature makes it a popular choice among poultry enthusiasts, although they can be bossy to other chickens.
Rhode Island Red	These deep red–hued chickens are robust and hardy, often lauded for being excellent egg layers. They have a friendly disposition and adapt well to various living conditions.
Sussex	Originating from England, Sussex chickens are versatile and come in various colors. With its beautiful, mottled feathers, the Speckled Sussex is particularly popular among poultry enthusiasts.
Wyandotte	With their broad, rounded bodies and diverse color patterns, Wyandottes are not only attractive but also productive, reliable layers. They're hardy and friendly, making them suitable for novice poultry keepers.

BANTAM BREEDS

Japanese Bantam	Distinguished by their short legs and upright tails, they are lively, sociable birds, often kept for ornamental purposes.
Pekin Bantam	These fluffy birds resemble the larger Cochin. They're docile and make great pets or show birds.
Sebright	These small, primarily ornamental, delicately laced birds are true bantams, meaning there's no large counterpart. They're active and have a confident nature.
Silkie	Unique in appearance and temperament, Silkies are known for their soft, fur-like feathers, bluish-black skin, and calm demeanor. They're often kept as ornamental or pet chickens.

GAME BREEDS

Modern Game	With their tall stature and long legs, Modern Game birds are primarily ornamental, bred for poultry shows rather than utility purposes.
Old English Game	Athletic and agile, these birds have a rich history linked to cockfighting (now illegal in many parts of the world, including the United States). They're muscular, active, and come in a variety of colors. They are raised now primarily for their exotic appearance.

RARE AND HERITAGE BREEDS

Araucana	Native to Chile, Araucanas are famous for laying blue eggs. They have a distinct appearance with tufted ears and a rumpless tail.
Croad Langshan	Originating from China, these tall birds have a unique U-shaped back profile. They're calm, dual-purpose birds known for their dark brown eggs.
Faverolle	Native to France, Faverolles are recognizable by their beard, muffs, and feathered legs. They're friendly, dual-purpose birds, often kept for meat and eggs.
Houdan	Another French breed, Houdans have a feathered crest and an extra toe. They're ornamental birds with a rich history linked to French cuisine.

EXOTIC AND ORNAMENTAL BREEDS

Phoenix	Renowned for their exceptionally long tails, Phoenix chickens are ornamental birds often kept for poultry shows.
Polish	Known for their striking feathered crests, Polish chickens are ornamental birds that add flair to any poultry flock.
Sumatra	Native to the Indonesian island of Sumatra, these birds are sleek with long, flowing tails and glossy black feathers. They're more ornamental, with a wild nature.

DUAL PURPOSE

Cornish	These broad-breasted birds are essential in the commercial meat industry, often crossed with other breeds to produce broilers.
New Hampshire Red	Developed from Rhode Island Reds, these birds are bred primarily for meat production but are also decent egg layers.

UTILITY BREEDS

Broilers or Meat Chickens	These are fast-growing chickens, with broad breasts and tender meat, specifically bred for food production.
Hybrid Layers	Chickens like ISA Brown, Red Star, and Black Star are primarily developed for high egg production, combining the best traits from various breeds.

For Southern cooking, especially classic dishes like Southern Fried Chicken (page 43), the best chickens are flavorful with a good meat-to-bone ratio. Traditionally, heritage breeds were used because of their deep flavor, but as commercial farming took over, broiler chickens became the go-to chickens due to their widespread availability and affordability.

The best chickens for Southern cooking are:

Broilers or meat chickens:
These young chickens are raised primarily for meat and are widely available. They're tender and have a good amount of meat, making them ideal for frying.

Cornish hen or Cornish cross:
This breed produces broad-breasted, meaty birds. Young birds are known as Cornish game hens, which are individual-sized and can be roasted whole.

Heritage breeds:
Breeds like the Sussex, Orpington, and Wyandotte are slower growing than commercial broilers but have more flavorful meat. They're ideal for dishes where the chicken's flavor needs to shine through.

Plymouth Rock (Barred Rock):
This older breed is known for its tasty meat, making it suitable for a range of Southern dishes.

Rhode Island Red:
Although more commonly associated with egg laying, older Rhode Island Reds can be used for stews and broths due to their flavorful meat.

When sourcing chicken for Southern cooking, consider how the chicken was raised. Free-range or pasture-raised chickens have a richer flavor than factory-farmed chicken as a result of their varied diet and more active lifestyle. However, they might have a firmer texture. For dishes where flavor is paramount, such as Chicken and Dumplings (page 47), opting for a free-range, organic bird is worth the extra cost. A standard broiler chicken is acceptable where the seasoning and crispy crust are central.

2

THE SOUTHERN ROOTS OF KOWBIRD

Chicken, Culture, and Community

In the South, the aroma of fried chicken wafting from a kitchen isn't just an indication of an anticipated meal, it's also the scent of heritage, family gatherings, and centuries of cultural evolution. For many, it represents Sunday afternoons at Grandma's house, church potlucks, or festive family reunions. The significance of chicken in Southern culture goes far beyond its taste. It's a testament to the art of making something extraordinary out of the ordinary.

I was aware of this rich history when I first envisioned Kowbird. Growing up, I witnessed the ritual of chicken preparation and cooking—how a simple bird, when combined with the right herbs, spices, and techniques, transforms into a delicacy that warmed hearts and made mouths water.

Kowbird is more than just a nod to my Southern roots, though. It is about building bridges, reviving communities, and fostering entrepreneurship. West Oakland was ripe with potential despite its challenges if you looked beyond its tough exterior. It's a community with a heart, yearning for something to instill pride and unity.

The journey to establish Kowbird was symbolic. Just as the South endured its share of challenges yet preserved its cultural legacy, I believed in transforming difficulties into opportunities. What better way to do that than to create a business that nourishes a community and enriches its fabric?

Entrepreneurship in challenging places isn't only about turning a profit. It's understanding the community's ethos, recognizing the gaps, and bridging them. You need to serve where you build. I didn't want Kowbird to be just another eatery. I envisioned a space where people from all walks of life share a table, meal, and stories. The restaurant is about creating employment, mentoring the next generation, and demonstrating that success isn't confined to ZIP codes.

My work extends beyond the kitchen to mentorship programs, community dialogues, and art showcases; Kowbird is a nexus of cultural exchange and empowerment. It emphasizes the importance of roots, remembering where you came from, and ensuring holistic, inclusive, community-driven growth.

The community response to Kowbird has been overwhelming. But the tantalizing chicken flavors weren't the only draw. The sense of belonging, the feeling that celebrates the inhabitants and essence of West Oakland, drew them there, too.

But why chicken? Chicken has an innate universality. Its versatility lies in its simplicity. In many ways, chicken reflects life in challenging neighborhoods—humble, often underestimated, and packed with potential. When treated with care, respect, and innovation, chicken is a source of immense joy, much like the community of West Oakland.

Today, Kowbird stands tall, a testament to entrepreneurial spirit and a beacon for what businesses can achieve when rooted in community.

KOWBIRD'S INSPIRATION
AND CULINARY JOURNEY

In the ever-expanding culinary world, many dishes possess a narrative woven with memories, traditions, and diverse influences. This convergence lies at the heart of Kowbird, deeply anchored in time-honored traditions, personal anecdotes, and a fervent love of food. From the vibrant streets of West Oakland to the rich culinary spirit of Nashville, Kowbird emerges as an expression of passion and dedication.

With its contribution of Nashville hot chicken to the culinary realm, Nashville is the foundation of my inspiration. The compelling story of Thornton Prince, where love and revenge gave rise to a city's culinary hallmark, etched a lasting imprint on me. The tale is a testament to the idea that unexpected events can produce iconic results. A sojourn to Prince's Hot Chicken Shack is transformative. The harmony of flavors, the electrifying spices, and the matchless art of frying set forth a gastronomic revelation. The dishes rise from simple origins, encapsulating the essence of place, history, and unique identity, and their legacy is carried on by a modern guardian in André Prince Jeffries. At the helm of Prince's Hot Chicken Shack since 1980, Andre's commitment to cherishing and perpetuating her family's culinary tradition is awe-inspiring.

Adding depth to this narrative is Bolton Matthews, former heir to Bolton Polk, the original patriarch of Nashville hot chicken. Matthews had an unwavering dedication to honoring his lineage and a passion for continuing the legacy of spicy fried chicken, all of which earned him a unique space in the culinary world. His venture, Bolton's Spicy Chicken and Fish, established in 1997, still stands as a proud testament to his family's rich heritage.

Venturing westward, the duo of Vincent and Arlene Williams at Honey's Kettle emerges as another source of inspiration. Their painstaking commitment to the art of frying and their community-driven approach to business meld seamlessly with the spirit of Kowbird.

In Los Angeles's vibrant landscape, Kim Prince's Hotville Chicken bridges the gap between Nashville's traditional heart and California's eclectic dynamism. This establishment, helmed by a descendant of the legendary Prince family, ensures the Prince legacy resonates, inspires, and evolves across generations and geography.

Similarly, Johnny Ray Zone's fresh twist on timeless flavors at Howlin' Rays penned an integral chapter in my culinary odyssey.

However, my vision for Kowbird extends beyond the fiery allure of hot chicken. At its core, it's a celebration of the ageless elegance of Southern fried chicken, especially within the idea of a sandwich. Kowbird's offerings, including the hot chicken sandwich, are not a nod to prevailing trends but a heartfelt tribute to institutions like Prince's and Bolton's enduring heritage.

Kowbird is an intricate tapestry woven with cherished memories, traditions, and inspirations. Nestled in West Oakland, it reflects a rich array of influences, transforming from a mere eatery to a story, an experience, and a tribute.

THE SIGNIFICANCE OF PRESERVING SOUTHERN CULINARY TRADITIONS

Southern cuisine is more than comfort food; it's a demonstration of history, culture, and soul. Rooted in tradition, forged by adversity, and seasoned with love, the dishes from the American South embody generations of stories, determination, and a deep sense of community. As the world becomes increasingly globalized and cultures merge, it's imperative to understand the importance of preserving Southern culinary traditions and honoring the heritage they represent.

Southern cooking has deep historical roots, influenced by Indigenous American, African, and European cultures. Indigenous Americans contributed corn, beans, and squash to the early settlers. Enslaved Africans brought to the American South during the transatlantic slave trade introduced okra, black-eyed peas, and deep-frying techniques. European settlers brought pork and beef—staples in Southern cuisine. The amalgamation of these cultures laid the foundation for gumbo, fried chicken, barbecue, and more.

Understanding the origins of these dishes pays homage to these cultures and highlights the adaptability of the region's people. They were not merely surviving but creating, innovating, and forging a legacy that continues to influence the global culinary scene.

Many Southern dishes—often labeled soul food—originated during times of hardship, particularly during slavery and the subsequent eras of segregation and economic disparity. Enslaved peoples often made do with the least desirable ingredients, which they transformed into nourishing and delicious meals with creativity and resourcefulness: pork intestines became chitterlings, pig's feet became a pickled delicacy, greens slow-cooked with ham hocks were sublime, and cornmeal transformed into grits.

By preserving these recipes, we honor them and pass on the traditions of crafting meals that not only feed the body but also nourish the soul.

Upholding these traditions ensures future generations understand their roots, creating a bridge between past and present, so stories are passed along with the meals. Cooking becomes a rite of passage, where elder generations impart wisdom, technique, and family lore to the younger ones.

Southern culinary traditions are not just about history and culture, but they also boost local economies. The South attracts tourists keen on experiencing its renowned culinary scene. Cities such as New Orleans, Nashville, and Charleston are celebrated for their unique food landscapes. Southern chefs enjoy international acclaim, showcasing their traditional dishes on global platforms, emphasizing the significance of preserving these culinary practices.

But Southern cuisine has evolved, reflecting modern values and influences. Chefs incorporate sustainable practices, source locally, and ensure ethical treatment of animals. Vegetarian and vegan variations of classic dishes emerge. This evolution doesn't dilute the essence of Southern culinary traditions but enriches it, making the food more inclusive and resonant with contemporary audiences.

The significance of preserving Southern culinary traditions goes beyond the plate. It's about upholding a legacy, recognizing the struggles and triumphs of past generations, and ensuring their stories, values, and innovations continue to inspire. Food is a universal language; Southern cuisine speaks of unity, endurance, and love. By honoring this rich heritage, the melodies of the past continue to harmonize with the present, crafting a symphony that will resonate for generations to come. Let's explore this incredible legacy.

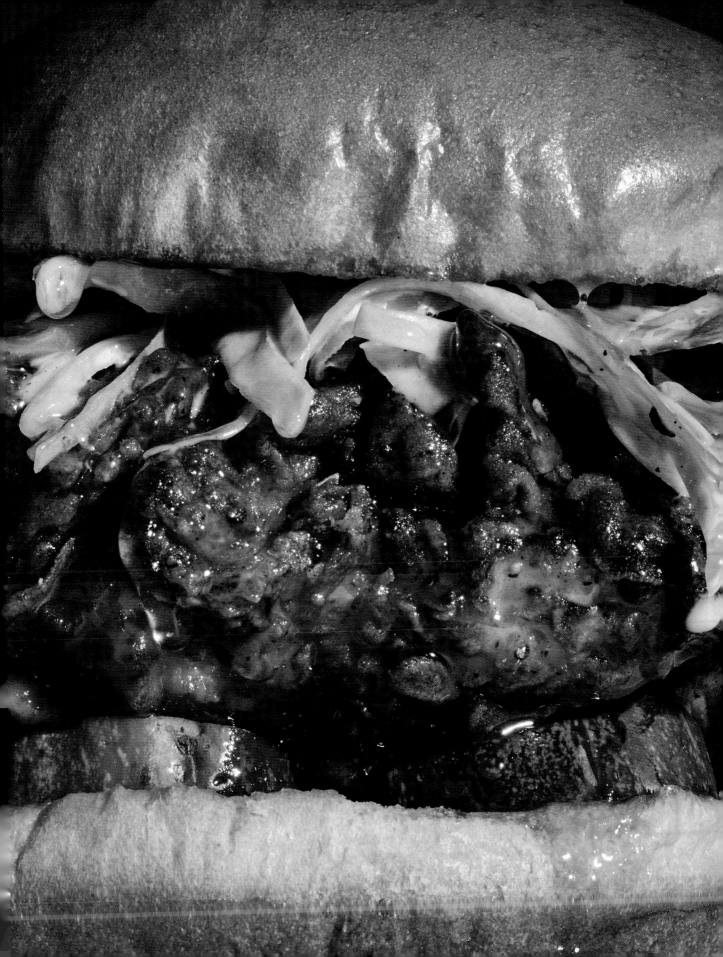

"In the ever-expanding culinary world, many dishes possess a narrative woven with memories, traditions, and diverse influences. This convergence lies at the heart of Kowbird."

3

CHICKEN MAINS

SOUTHERN FRIED CHICKEN

Yield: Serves 4 | Prep time: 15 minutes, plus at least 2 hours marinating time | Cook time: 45 minutes

Imagine a sun-kissed porch in the Deep South, the echo of distant family laughter. This chicken isn't just a dish, it's a tradition. It speaks of Sunday dinners, where families gathered, united over the golden, crispy crust and tender meat. Each bite carries the memories and spirit of Southern hospitality. As you savor it, taste the history and the love of generations past, and continue the legacy.

1 (4-pound, or 1.8 kg) whole chicken, cut into pieces

2 cups (480 ml) buttermilk

2 cups (248 g) all-purpose flour

2 teaspoons paprika

1 teaspoon garlic powder

1 teaspoon onion powder

½ teaspoon cayenne pepper

Salt

Freshly ground black pepper

Vegetable oil or lard, for frying

1. In a large bowl, combine the chicken pieces and buttermilk. Cover and refrigerate to marinate for at least 2 hours, or overnight.

2. In another large bowl, whisk the flour, paprika, garlic powder, onion powder, cayenne, and salt and black pepper to taste until blended.

3. In a deep-fryer or large skillet over medium heat, heat 3 inches (7.5 cm) of oil to 350°F (177°C).

4. Remove the chicken from the marinade and dredge each chicken in the flour mixture, ensuring it's well coated.

5. Working in batches, carefully add the chicken to the hot oil and fry for 8 to 10 minutes for the smaller pieces, or 13 to 15 minutes for larger pieces, until golden brown and cooked through, with an internal temperature of 165°F (73°C). Transfer the fried chicken to a wire rack to drain.

6. Serve warm. Refrigerate leftover chicken in an airtight container for up to 5 days.

WHITE WINE CHICKEN

Yield: Serves 4 to 6 | Prep time: 15 minutes | Cook time: 55 minutes

When creating a simmering pot of this French culinary classic, called coq au vin blanc *in French, you're not just crafting a meal but becoming part of a rich tapestry woven through generations, cultures, and shared moments. The marriage of chicken and wine is as eternal as the gently rolling vineyards from which the ingredients came. Serve over mashed potatoes or rice for a true delight to enjoy with family and loved ones.*

4 bacon slices, diced

3 tablespoons (42 g) butter or (45 ml) olive oil

8 bone-in, skin-on chicken pieces (thighs, breasts, drumsticks)

1 cup (130 g) peeled pearl onions

1 cup (70 g) sliced mushrooms

3 garlic cloves, minced

2 cups (480 ml) dry white wine (such as Chardonnay)

2 cups (480 ml) chicken broth

2 thyme sprigs

1 bay leaf

Salt

Freshly ground black pepper

1. In a large pot or Dutch oven over medium heat, cook the bacon for about 5 minutes until crispy. With a slotted spoon, transfer the bacon to a large plate, leaving the bacon fat in the pan.

2. Add the butter to the pot to melt. Carefully add the chicken pieces and cook for about 6 minutes, turning, until browned on all sides. Transfer the chicken to the plate with the bacon.

3. Add the onions, mushrooms, and garlic to the remaining fat in the pan and sauté for about 4 minutes until soft.

4. Pour in the white wine to deglaze the pan, scraping up any browned bits from the bottom. Return the chicken and bacon to the pot.

5. Add the broth, thyme, bay leaf, and salt and pepper to taste. Bring to a boil, reduce the heat to low, cover the pan, and simmer for 30 to 40 minutes, or until the chicken is cooked through, with an internal temperature of 165°F (73°C).

6. Remove and discard the thyme and bay leaf before serving the chicken with the sauce spooned over the top.

7. Refrigerate leftovers in an airtight container for up to 3 days.

CHICKEN AND DUMPLINGS

Yield: Serves 4 to 6 | Prep time: 15 minutes | Cook time: 55 minutes

This comfort food staple is steeped in homespun heritage, connecting you to more than one hundred years of tradition. In crafting this meal of tender dumplings and savory chicken, you're feeding the body and nourishing the soul.

4 tablespoons (½ stick, or 56 g) unsalted butter

1 onion, diced

2 celery stalks, chopped

2 carrots, chopped

8 bone-in, skin-on chicken pieces (thighs, breasts, drumsticks)

8 cups (1.9 L) chicken broth

2 cups (248 g) all-purpose flour

2 tablespoons (8 g) chopped fresh parsley, plus more for garnish

1 tablespoon (14 g) baking powder

Salt

Freshly ground black pepper

1 cup (240 ml) milk

1. In a large pot over medium heat, melt the butter. Add the onion, celery, and carrots and sauté for about 6 minutes until softened.

2. Add the chicken pieces, pour in the broth, and bring the liquid to a boil. Reduce the heat to low and simmer for 30 to 40 minutes, or until the chicken is cooked through, with an internal temperature of 165°F (73°C).

3. In a small bowl, whisk the flour, parsley, baking powder, and salt and pepper to taste to blend. Pour in the milk and whisk until just combined. Drop tablespoonfuls of the dumpling dough into the simmering pot. Cover the pot and simmer for 15 minutes, or until the dumplings are cooked through and no longer doughy.

4. Remove the chicken bones, if desired, before serving. Garnish with parsley.

5. Refrigerate leftovers in an airtight container for 3 to 5 days.

CREOLE CHICKEN JAMBALAYA

Yield: Serves 4 to 6 | Prep time: 15 minutes | Cook time: 40 minutes

As the piquant aroma fills the air and the pot bubbles with promise, know you're part of a mélange of cultures. Jambalaya's lively spices and combination of ingredients speak of Louisiana's spirited festivals, traditions, and the joie de vivre of the South.

2 tablespoons (30 ml) vegetable oil

4 (6-ounce, or 170 g) boneless, skinless chicken thighs, diced

1 cup (138 g) sliced andouille sausage

1 onion, finely chopped

1 green bell pepper, diced

2 celery stalks, chopped

3 garlic cloves, minced

2 teaspoons Cajun Seasoning (page 154), or store-bought

2 cups (400 g) white rice

2 tomatoes, diced

4 cups (960 ml) chicken stock

3 scallions, white and green parts, sliced

Salt

Freshly ground black pepper

1. In a large pot or Dutch oven over medium heat, heat the oil. Add the chicken and sausage and cook for 5 minutes until browned.

2. Add the onion, bell pepper, and celery and sauté for about 4 minutes until softened.

3. Stir in the garlic and Cajun seasoning and cook for 2 minutes.

4. Stir in the rice, ensuring each grain is coated in the seasoned mixture.

5. Add the tomatoes and stock and bring the liquid to a boil. Reduce the heat to low, cover the pan, and simmer for 20 to 25 minutes, or until the rice is cooked through and has absorbed the stock.

6. Stir in the scallions. Taste and season with salt and pepper.

7. Serve the jambalaya warm. Refrigerate leftovers in an airtight container for 3 to 5 days.

CHICKEN AND WAFFLES

Yield: Serves 4 to 6 | Prep time: 10 minutes
Cook time: 20 minutes, plus about 12 minutes per batch of Southern Fried Chicken

My first taste of this pairing was at Roscoe's in Inglewood, California, where the golden waffles and crispy fried chicken seemed more than just food; they were a revelation. Each bite was the richly woven fabric of Los Angeles culture, representing stories of soulful kitchens, sunlit boulevards, and the heartbeat of a city that celebrates contrasts.

2 cups (248 g) all-purpose flour

2 teaspoons baking powder

½ teaspoon salt

2 large eggs, beaten

1¾ cups (420 ml) milk

½ cup (120 ml) vegetable oil or melted butter

1 recipe cooked Southern Fried Chicken (page 43), still warm

Maple syrup, for serving

1. Preheat a waffle iron following the manufacturer's instructions.

2. In a medium bowl, whisk the flour, baking powder, and salt to blend.

3. In another medium bowl, whisk the eggs, milk, and oil until combined.

4. Add the wet ingredients to the dry ingredients and whisk until just combined. Pour the batter into the waffle iron following the manufacturer's recommendations and cook until golden brown. Repeat until all the batter is used.

5. Serve the warm fried chicken on top of the waffles with a generous drizzle of maple syrup.

6. Refrigerate leftovers in separate airtight containers for up to 4 days.

NASHVILLE HOT CHICKEN

Yield: Serves 4 to 6 | Prep time: 10 minutes
Cook time: About 12 minutes per batch of Southern Fried Chicken

Inspired by the famed Prince family, this spicy dish tells a tale of passion, pride, and the sweet revenge of a betrayed woman. Each crispy bite, lacquered in its signature hot oil, connects us to the vibrant rhythms of Music City. Dive in and taste not just the heat but the history of a family that turned heartbreak into a culinary tradition.

½ cup (115 g) unsalted butter

3 tablespoons (16 g) cayenne pepper (adjust to taste)

2 tablespoons (28 g) brown sugar

2 teaspoons (13 g) coarse kosher salt

2 teaspoons (4 g) ground black pepper

2 teaspoons (6 g) garlic powder

1 teaspoon smoked paprika

1 tablespoon (20 g) honey, optional

2 tablespoons (30 ml) pickle juice from your favorite pickles

½ teaspoon onion powder

¼ teaspoon ghost pepper powder, if you have it, or additional cayenne

1 recipe cooked Southern Fried Chicken (page 43), still warm

Sliced white bread, for serving

Pickles, for serving

1. Combine the butter, cayenne pepper, brown sugar, salt, pepper, garlic powder, paprika, honey (if you are using it), pickle juice, onion powder, and ghost pepper powder (or additional cayenne) in a heavy-bottom saucepan. Stir over low heat until combined; do not heat over high heat, which will give the sugars a hard, candy-like consistency. The mixture will not be smooth.

2. Fry the chicken, if not already fried. Stir the hot sauce so that it is evenly combined and brush it liberally over all sides of the warm chicken pieces immediately after frying.

3. Serve the hot chicken on the bread slices with a pile of pickles on the side.

4. Refrigerate leftover chicken and sauce in separate airtight containers for up to 3 days.

BARBECUE CHICKEN

Yield: Serves 4 to 6 | Prep time: 10 minutes | Cook time: 35 minutes

My trusty smoker, Lucille, and I shared countless sunrises—her smoke dancing in the early light as I stoked her embers and prepared for another day. True barbecue chicken is born from patience and time. Each piece tells a story, as the wood's whisper and the fire's glow impart secrets only a pitmaster knows. With every bite, you'll taste more than chicken; I've poured the soul of the South and my love for Lucille into every smoky morsel.

8 bone-in, skin-on chicken pieces (thighs, breasts, drumsticks)

2 tablespoons (18 g) Southern Barbecue Rub (page 158)

Salt

Freshly ground black pepper

1 cup (250 g) barbecue sauce

2 tablespoons (30 ml) apple cider vinegar

1. Preheat a grill or the oven to medium-high heat (375°F, or 190.5°C, or gas mark 5). Season the chicken pieces with the rub and salt and pepper to taste.

2. Grill the chicken, turning occasionally, for 20 to 25 minutes, or until it is almost cooked through, with an internal temperature of about 155°F (68°C).

3. In a small bowl, stir together the barbecue sauce and vinegar. Brush the mixture onto the chicken pieces. Continue to cook for 10 minutes, brushing with more sauce and turning the pieces a couple of times, until the chicken is glazed and fully cooked, with an internal temperature of 165°F (73°C).

4. Serve warm. Refrigerate leftover chicken in an airtight container for up to 3 days.

My Mother's
SMOTHERED CHICKEN

Yield: Serves 4 to 6 | Prep time: 15 minutes | Cook time: 45 minutes

In our humble kitchen, the aroma of this dish was a tribute to my mother's ingenuity. Inspired by grandparents Elsie and Isaiah, my mother would weave magic from simple ingredients, turning them into a meal bursting with love and memories. Each bite of seasoned meat and rich gravy reminded me of my relatives' resourcefulness, stories of making do with little, yet creating so much.

3 tablespoons (42 g) butter or (45 ml) vegetable oil

8 bone-in, skin-on chicken pieces (thighs, breasts, drumsticks)

1 large onion, sliced

1 bell pepper (any color), sliced

3 garlic cloves, minced

3 tablespoons (23 g) all-purpose flour

2 cups (480 ml) chicken broth

1 teaspoon Cajun Seasoning (page 154) or Creole Seasoning (page 155), or store-bought

Salt

Freshly ground black pepper

Cooked mashed potatoes or rice, for serving

1. In a large skillet over medium heat, melt the butter. Add the chicken pieces and cook for about 6 minutes, turning, until browned on all sides. Transfer the chicken to a plate.

2. In the same skillet, combine the onion, bell pepper, and garlic. Sauté for about 4 minutes until softened.

3. Stir in the flour and cook for 2 minutes.

4. Gradually whisk in the broth, ensuring no lumps form.

5. Return the chicken to the skillet and add the seasoning and salt and pepper to taste. Cover the skillet and simmer for 25 to 30 minutes, or until the chicken is cooked through, with an internal temperature of 165°F (73°C), and the sauce has thickened.

6. Serve warm over the mashed potatoes.

7. Refrigerate leftovers in an airtight container for up to 3 days.

ROASTED PARMESAN CHICKEN

Yield: Serves 4 | Prep time: 15 minutes | Cook time: 30 minutes

When serving this golden-crusted delight to your family, you pay homage to timeless Italian craftsmanship. Combining robust Parmesan with delicate herbs conjures memories of Old World kitchens where every ingredient builds flavor. Each mouthful captures the essence of family and the simple joy of sharing a meal.

½ cup (50 g) grated Parmesan cheese

½ cup (60 g) bread crumbs

1 teaspoon garlic powder

1 teaspoon dried basil or oregano

Salt

Freshly ground black pepper

4 (6-ounce, or 170 g) bone-in, skin-on chicken breasts or thighs

3 tablespoons (45 ml) olive oil or melted butter

1. Preheat the oven to 375°F (190.5°C, or gas mark 5).

2. In a medium bowl, whisk the Parmesan, bread crumbs, garlic powder, basil, and salt and pepper to taste to blend.

3. Generously brush each chicken piece with oil.

4. Dredge the chicken in the bread crumb mixture, ensuring it's well coated and pressing the mixture onto the chicken to adhere. Arrange the coated chicken pieces on a baking sheet.

5. Bake for 40 to 45 minutes, or until the chicken is golden brown and fully cooked through, with an internal temperature of 165°F (73°C).

6. Serve warm, complemented by your choice of side dishes.

7. Refrigerate leftovers in an airtight container for up to 3 days.

CHICKEN POTPIE
with Corn Bread Topping

Yield: Serves 4 | Prep time: 20 minutes | Cook time: 45 minutes

When I was a child, frozen potpies hinted at comfort and convenience but, somehow, missed the mark on flavor. As this dish emerges from the oven, the golden corn bread crust breathes new life into that old familiar. Beneath the crust lies a savory filling of chicken and vegetables reminiscent of childhood, yet elevated. It's a journey from simple packaged beginnings to deep culinary exploration while retaining the cherished memories of that first delightful bite.

For the filling

4 tablespoons (½ stick, or 56 g) unsalted butter

½ cup (80 g) chopped onion

½ cup (50 g) chopped celery

¼ cup (31 g) all-purpose flour

2 cups (480 ml) chicken broth

½ cup (120 ml) cream or milk

2 cups (280 g) diced cooked chicken

1 cup (130 g) diced carrot

1 cup (150 g) fresh or frozen peas

Salt

Freshly ground black pepper

For the corn bread topping

1 cup (140 g) cornmeal

1 cup (124 g) all-purpose flour

2 tablespoons (25 g) sugar

4 teaspoons (18 g) baking powder

2 large eggs

1 cup (240 ml) milk

¼ cup (60 ml) melted butter

To make the filling

1. Preheat the oven to 400°F (204°C, or gas mark 6).

2. In a large skillet over medium heat, melt the butter. Add the onion and celery and sauté for about 4 minutes until translucent. Stir in the flour to create a roux and slowly whisk in the broth and milk. Bring the sauce to a simmer and let simmer for 3 to 4 minutes so that the roux thickens.

3. Add the chicken, carrot, and peas. Season with salt and pepper to taste and pour the mixture into a 10-inch (25 cm) baking dish.

To make the corn bread topping

4. In a medium bowl, whisk the cornmeal, flour, sugar, and baking powder to blend. Whisk in the eggs, milk, and melted butter. Pour the topping over the chicken filling.

5. Bake for 25 to 30 minutes, or until the filling is bubbling and the corn bread is golden brown.

6. Refrigerate leftovers in an airtight container for up to 3 days.

CHICKEN GUMBO
with Andouille Sausage

Yield: Serves 4 | Prep time: 20 minutes | Cook time: 1 hour and 35 minutes

Each spoonful of this rich stew is a trip down the bayou, where generational traditions simmer gently in the pot. The depth of the chicken flavor melds seamlessly with the smoky kick of andouille, creating a harmonious blend that speaks of sultry Southern nights and the undeniable spirit of Creole and Cajun kitchens. Dive in and let the history and warmth of this dish transport you.

¼ cup (31 g) all-purpose flour

¼ cup (60 ml) vegetable oil

½ cup (80 g) chopped onion

½ cup (75 g) chopped green bell pepper

½ cup (50 g) chopped celery

4 garlic cloves, minced

4 cups (960 ml) chicken stock

1 (14-ounce, or 395 g) can diced tomatoes, undrained

2 (6-ounce, or 170 g) boneless, skinless chicken breasts, diced

1 pound (454 g) andouille sausage, sliced

2 teaspoons Cajun Seasoning (page 154), or store-bought

1 teaspoon dried thyme

2 bay leaves

Salt

Freshly ground black pepper

½ cup (50 g) sliced fresh okra (optional)

Cooked white rice, for serving

4 scallions, white and green parts, sliced

1. In a large pot, whisk the flour and oil until smooth to create a roux. Place the pot over medium-low heat and cook, whisking occasionally, for about 30 minutes, or until the mixture turns a dark brown color.

2. Add the onion, bell pepper, and celery and cook for about 4 minutes until softened. Add the garlic and cook for 1 minute.

3. Increase the heat to medium and add the stock, diced tomatoes and their juices, chicken, andouille, Cajun seasoning, thyme, and bay leaves. Bring to a boil, then reduce the heat to low, and simmer the stew for 1 hour. Add the okra (if using) during the last 20 minutes of cooking.

4. Season with salt and pepper to taste and serve the gumbo hot over white rice. Garnish with scallions.

5. Refrigerate leftovers in an airtight container for up to 3 days.

BOURBON-GLAZED CHICKEN

Yield: Serves 4 | Prep time: 10 minutes | Cook time: 30 minutes

This creation is a marriage of deep Southern American traditions and the memory of the joyous gatherings of my youth. As the golden glaze with its hints of smoky bourbon caramelizes on the succulent chicken, I think of warm evenings and laughter echoing beneath the wide canopy of oak trees. This perfectly prepared chicken honors Southern elegance, the magic of family recipes, and those cherished moments when the comforts of food and good company intertwine.

½ cup (120 ml) bourbon

½ cup (120 g) packed brown sugar

2 tablespoons (30 ml) soy sauce

2 garlic cloves, minced

1 teaspoon minced peeled fresh ginger

4 (6-ounce, or 170 g) bone-in, skin-on chicken breasts or thighs

Salt

Freshly ground black pepper

1. Preheat the oven to 375°F (190.5°C, or gas mark 5).

2. In a medium saucepan, combine the bourbon, brown sugar, soy sauce, garlic, and ginger. Place the pan over high heat and bring the sauce to a boil, then reduce the heat to low, and simmer for 8 to 10 minutes until the mixture thickens into a glaze.

3. Season the chicken with salt and pepper to taste and brush each piece with the bourbon glaze. Place the chicken on a baking sheet and bake for 30 to 35 minutes for thighs and 40 to 45 minutes for breasts, basting occasionally with more glaze, until the chicken is cooked through, with an internal temperature of 165°F (73°C).

4. Refrigerate leftovers in an airtight container for up to 3 days.

LEMON HERB GRILLED CHICKEN

Yield: Serves 4 | Prep time: 15 minutes, plus 2 hours marinating time | Cook time: 20 minutes

Putting this recipe together carries me back to my grandmother's fragrant herb garden. The vibrant zing of freshly squeezed lemons pairs with aromatic fresh herbs, enveloping the chicken in a celebration of flavors. It's summer on a plate—a reminder of family barbecues and the simple pleasure of biting into a juicy piece of chicken that was kissed by the char of the grill and seasoned by loving hands.

Grated zest of 2 lemons

Juice of 2 lemons

2 tablespoons (30 ml) olive oil

1 tablespoon (2 g) chopped
    fresh rosemary

1 tablespoon (2.5 g) chopped
    fresh thyme

2 garlic cloves, minced

Salt

Freshly ground black pepper

4 (4-ounce, or 115 g) bone-in,
    skin-on chicken breasts
    or thighs

1. In a medium bowl, stir together the lemon zest, lemon juice, oil, rosemary, thyme, garlic, and salt and pepper to taste until well combined. Add the chicken, turning to coat. Cover and refrigerate to marinate for at least 2 hours.

2. Preheat a grill to medium-high heat (about 375°F, or 190.5°C).

3. Place the chicken on the grill and cook for 8 to 10 minutes per side, or until fully cooked, with an internal temperature of 165°F (73°C).

4. Refrigerate leftovers in an airtight container for up to 3 days.

Georgia Peach
CHICKEN THIGHS

Yield: Serves 4 to 6 | Prep time: 15 minutes | Cook time: 45 minutes

Imagine a time when life moved a tad more slowly, in a quaint little town where, after Sunday service, a preacher's wife serves up these succulent treasures. The blend of juicy peaches and a hint of spice glazes each chicken thigh with pure perfection. It's a tender homage to faith, community, and Georgia's bounty.

---

2 ripe peaches, pitted and sliced

¼ cup (60 g) packed brown sugar

¼ cup (60 ml) balsamic vinegar

¼ teaspoon ground cinnamon

4 (5-ounce, or 140 g) bone-in, skin-on chicken thighs

Salt

Freshly ground black pepper

1. Preheat the oven to 400°F (204°C, or gas mark 6).

2. In a saucepan over medium heat, stir together the peaches, brown sugar, vinegar, and cinnamon. Cook for about 8 minutes until the peaches are soft and the sauce has thickened.

3. Season the chicken thighs with salt and pepper to taste and place them in a 10-inch (25 cm) baking dish. Top with the peach mixture.

4. Bake the chicken for 30 to 35 minutes, or until the chicken is cooked through, with an internal temperature of 165°F (73°C).

5. Refrigerate leftovers in an airtight container for up to 3 days.

SOUTHERN CHICKEN SALAD
with Pecans

Yield: Serves 4 to 6 | **Prep time: 15 minutes, plus 2 hours chilling time**

Every Southern gathering has its staples, but something about this salad always drew me in as a child. When I make it today, it's not just tender chicken chunks or golden, buttery pecans that delight me; instead, it's the scrapbook of memories found into each bite. Enjoy on a bed of greens or between slices of your favorite bread.

2 cups (280 g) diced cooked chicken

½ cup (115 g) mayonnaise

¼ cup (27.5 g) chopped pecans

¼ cup (25 g) chopped celery

¼ cup (38 g) halved red grapes

1 teaspoon fresh lemon juice

Salt

Freshly ground black pepper

1. In a large bowl, combine the chicken, mayonnaise, pecans, celery, grapes, lemon juice, and salt and pepper to taste. Stir well so all the ingredients are coated.

2. Cover and refrigerate the salad for at least 2 hours before serving.

3. Refrigerate leftovers in an airtight container for up to 3 days.

CHICKEN ÉTOUFFÉE

Yield: Serves 4 to 6 | **Prep time: 15 minutes** | **Cook time: 1 hour and 35 minutes**

Rich roux and the aromatic trinity of bell pepper, onion, and celery speak of old Louisiana kitchens where Creole magic was performed. Every time this dish simmers on my stove, I'm transported to bayou evenings, where the air is thick with anticipation. Cooking the roux to the perfect golden brown is time well spent, especially when that time well used connects you to the traditions of a vibrant culture.

4 tablespoons (½ stick, or 56 g) unsalted butter

½ cup (80 g) chopped onion

½ cup (75 g) chopped green bell pepper

½ cup (50 g) chopped celery

2 garlic cloves, minced

¼ cup (31 g) all-purpose flour

2 cups (480 ml) chicken broth

2 cups (300 g) diced raw chicken

2 teaspoons Cajun Seasoning (page 154) or Creole Seasoning (page 155), or store-bought

1 bay leaf

Salt

Freshly ground black pepper

Cooked white rice, for serving

Scallions, white and green parts, sliced, for garnish

1. In a large pot over medium-high heat, melt the butter. Add the onion, bell pepper, and celery and sauté for about 4 minutes until softened. Add the garlic and cook for 1 to 2 minutes until fragrant.

2. Whisk in the flour to create a roux and cook, whisking often, for about 45 minutes until golden brown.

3. Slowly pour in the broth, stirring continuously to prevent lumps. Add the chicken, Cajun seasoning, bay leaf, and salt and pepper to taste. Bring the mixture to a simmer, reduce the heat to low, and simmer for 30 minutes.

4. Serve the étouffée over white rice and garnish with scallions.

5. Refrigerate leftovers in an airtight container for up to 3 days.

CHICKEN FRIED CHICKEN
with Cream Gravy

Yield: Serves 4 to 6 | Prep time: 15 minutes | Cook time: 30 minutes

Chicken fried chicken is the heart and soul of Southern comfort with its golden crust and decadent cream gravy. As the gravy blankets the crispy chicken, think of the countless hands that crafted this delicacy, passing the cooking method from generation to generation. This meal bridges today and a time when life's pleasures were simple and deeply savored.

For the chicken fried chicken

4 (6-ounce, or 170 g) boneless, skinless chicken breasts, pounded thin

1 teaspoon garlic powder

1 teaspoon onion powder

Salt

Freshly ground black pepper

1 cup (124 g) all-purpose flour

2 large eggs, beaten

Vegetable oil, for frying

For the cream gravy

2 tablespoons (28 g) unsalted butter

2 tablespoons (15.5 g) all-purpose flour

2 cups (480 ml) milk

Salt

Freshly ground black pepper

To make the chicken fried chicken

1. Season the chicken all over with the garlic powder, onion powder, and salt and pepper to taste.

2. Place the flour in a medium bowl, next to the eggs in another medium bowl. Stir the milk into the eggs. Dredge the chicken in the flour, then in the egg mixture, and again in the flour.

3. In a large skillet over medium heat, heat 3 inches (7 cm) of oil until it reaches 350°F (177°C).

4. Carefully add the chicken to the hot oil and fry for 10 to 12 minutes, turning once, until golden brown and fully cooked, with an internal temperature of 165°F (73°C).

5. Transfer the chicken to paper towels to drain.

To make the gravy

6. In a medium saucepan over medium heat, melt the butter. Whisk in the flour and cook for 1 minute. While whisking, slowly pour in the milk. Cook for 8 to 10 minutes until the gravy thickens. Season with salt and pepper to taste.

7. Serve the fried chicken with the hot gravy.

8. Refrigerate leftovers in separate airtight containers for up to 3 days.

BLACKENED CHICKEN
with Remoulade Sauce

Yield: Serves 4 | **Prep time: 15 minutes** | **Cook time: 20 minutes**

Fire and flavors hailing from the vibrant New Orleans streets kiss this aromatic chicken. With each sizzling mouthful, envision jazz melodies floating through the air, punctuated by laughter and clinking glasses. The remoulade sauce—creamy, tangy, with a hint of zest—blends French sophistication with Creole soul and the perfect cooling accompaniment.

2 tablespoons (14 g) paprika

1 tablespoon (5 g) cayenne pepper

1 tablespoon (7 g) onion powder

1 tablespoon (9 g) garlic powder

1 teaspoon dried thyme

Salt

Freshly ground black pepper

4 (6-ounce, or 170 g) bone-in, skin-on chicken breasts

2 tablespoons (30 ml) vegetable oil

½ recipe Remoulade Sauce (page 138)

1. In a small bowl, stir together the paprika, cayenne, onion powder, garlic powder, thyme, and salt and black pepper to taste. Rub the mixture onto the chicken breasts.

2. In a large skillet over high heat, heat the oil until it shimmers. Add the chicken and cook for about 20 minutes, turning once, until blackened and cooked through, with an internal temperature of 165°F (73°C).

3. Serve the chicken with the remoulade sauce.

4. Refrigerate leftovers in separate airtight containers for up to 3 days.

CHICKEN STUFFED
with Pimento Cheese

Yield: Serves 4 | Prep time: 15 minutes | Cook time: 30 minutes

Chicken stuffed with pimento cheese is more than a mere entrée—it's a nostalgic embrace. This dish evokes easy Southern afternoons, porch swings, and the comforting chatter of loved ones. Surprisingly, though, in light of how popular and distinctly Southern this dish is now, it was not common in the South until after World War II. As you slice into this succulent chicken, molten pimento cheese oozes out—scoop up every bite.

4 (6-ounce, or 170 g) boneless, skinless chicken breasts

1 cup (248 g) pimento cheese

Salt

Freshly ground black pepper

½ cup (58 g) bread crumbs

2 tablespoons (30 ml) melted butter

1. Preheat the oven to 375°F (190.5°C, or gas mark 5).

2. Make a pocket in each chicken breast by cutting a slit in one side, without cutting all the way through. Stuff the cavities with the pimento cheese, dividing it evenly.

3. Season the chicken all over with salt and pepper to taste and roll the pieces in the bread crumbs. Place the breasts on a baking sheet and drizzle with melted butter.

4. Bake the chicken for 25 to 30 minutes, or until it is cooked through, with an internal temperature of 165°F (73°C).

5. Refrigerate leftovers in an airtight container for 3 to 5 days.

CHICKEN BRUNSWICK STEW

Yield: Serves 4 to 6 | Prep time: 15 minutes | Cook time: 55 minutes

Brunswick stew is communal Southern cooking at its finest. Originating from gatherings around large pots in Brunswick County, townsfolk contributed what they had, creating a nourishing pot of flavors and histories. Chicken is the star, complemented by a medley of vegetables and spices, and the combination carries the warmth of community.

2 tablespoons (30 ml) vegetable oil

1 onion, chopped

2 garlic cloves, minced

2 (6-ounce, or 170 g) boneless, skinless chicken breasts, diced

4 cups (960 ml) chicken broth

1 (14-ounce, or 395 g) can diced tomatoes, undrained

1 (14-ounce, or 395 g) can corn, drained

1 (14-ounce, or 395 g) can lima beans, drained

½ teaspoon smoked paprika

Salt

Freshly ground black pepper

1. In a large pot over medium-high heat, heat the oil until it's shimmering. Add the onion and garlic and sauté for about 3 minutes until softened.

2. Add the chicken and cook for about 5 minutes, turning, until browned on all sides.

3. Stir in the broth, diced tomatoes and their juices, corn, lima beans, smoked paprika, and salt and pepper to taste. Bring the stew to a boil, reduce the heat to low, and simmer for 30 to 40 minutes, or until the chicken is tender and no longer pink.

4. Serve the stew hot.

5. Refrigerate leftovers in an airtight container for 3 to 5 days.

Aunt Olivia's
CHICKEN SALAD

Yield: Serves 4 | Prep time: 15 minutes, plus 1 hour chilling time

My Aunt Olivia made the most divine chicken salad in the heart of Ponchatoula, Louisiana, where the air is perfumed with the scent of strawberries and the Spanish moss drapes ancient oaks. Her secret wasn't the ingredients but the love folded into each batch. Whipping up this salad, I can imagine myself in her cozy kitchen, listening to her stories of days gone by.

2 cups (280 g) diced cooked chicken

½ cup (50 g) chopped celery

¼ cup (40 g) diced red onion

⅓ cup (75 g) mayonnaise

1 tablespoon (15 g) Dijon mustard

2 tablespoons (8 g) chopped fresh dill

Salt

Freshly ground black pepper

¼ cup (23 g) sliced almonds (optional)

1. In a medium bowl, combine the chicken, celery, onion, mayonnaise, mustard, dill, and salt and pepper to taste. Stir well so all the ingredients are coated. Taste and add more salt and pepper, as needed.

2. Cover and refrigerate the salad for at least 1 hour before serving.

3. Refrigerate leftovers in an airtight container for 3 to 5 days.

FRIED GIZZARDS

Yield: Serves 4 to 6 | Prep time: 15 minutes, plus at least 2 hours marinating time
Cook time: 25 minutes

Fried gizzards are a throwback to my childhood when simplicity reigned supreme.
Crunchy on the outside and tender inside, these little gems are more than a Southern treat;
they're a callback to when every part of the bird was used. Long before "nose to tail" eating became
a trend, people knew the value of not wasting a morsel. So, step outside your comfort zone
and enjoy this often-overlooked delicacy.

---

1 pound (454 g) chicken gizzards, cleaned

1 cup (240 ml) buttermilk

1 cup (124 g) all-purpose flour

1 teaspoon paprika

1 teaspoon garlic powder

Salt

Freshly ground black pepper

Vegetable oil, for frying

1. In a medium bowl, combine the gizzards and buttermilk, turning to coat. Cover and refrigerate to marinate for at least 2 hours.

2. In another medium bowl, whisk the flour, paprika, garlic powder, and salt and pepper to taste to blend.

3. In a medium skillet over medium-high heat, heat 2 inches (5 cm) of oil until it reaches 350°F (177°C).

4. Remove the gizzards from the marinade, dredge them in the flour mixture, and carefully add them to the hot oil. Fry for about 25 minutes, turning once, until they are golden brown and cooked through, with an internal temperature of 165°F (73°C). Transfer to paper towels to drain.

GIBLETS AND GRITS

Yield: Serves 4 to 6 | Prep time: 10 minutes | Cook time: 1 hour and 5 minutes

In the heart of the South, giblets and grits hold a special place. This dish is a patchwork of humble ingredients, harkening to ancestors who crafted flavorful meals from simple means. It's a tribute to resourcefulness, tradition, and the timeless bond of family gathered around a shared table.

1 pound (454 g) chicken giblets, chopped

4 cups (960 ml) water

1 cup (140 g) grits

½ cup (60 g) grated Cheddar cheese

2 tablespoons (28 g) butter

Salt

Freshly ground black pepper

1. Place the giblets in a medium saucepan and cover with 2 inches (5 cm) of water. Place the pan over medium-high heat and bring the giblets to a boil. Cook for about 45 minutes until tender.

2. In a large saucepan, bring the water to a boil and stir in the grits. Reduce the heat to low and cook for about 20 minutes until soft. Remove the grits from the heat and stir in the cheese, butter, and salt and pepper to taste.

3. Serve the giblets over the cheesy grits.

4. Refrigerate leftovers in separate airtight containers for up to 3 days.

Kowbird Honey Butter
FRIED CHICKEN SANDWICH

Yield: Serves 2 | Prep time: 10 minutes, plus at least 2 hours marinating time | Cook time: 15 minutes

In the bustling heart of the city, where dreams manifest in the most unexpected corners, Kowbird was born. It all began as a modest pop-up. Opening the doors to our restaurant, the vision I held close was this incredible sandwich. Inspired by the rich traditions of Horn Barbecue, every bite molds the sweetness of honey with the golden crunch of perfectly fried chicken. It's more than a sandwich; it's the realization of a dream, served with a side of ambition and drizzled in determination.

---

2 (6-ounce, or 170 g) boneless, skinless chicken breasts, pounded thin (You can also use large boneless chicken thighs.)

1 cup (240 ml) buttermilk

2 cups (248 g) all-purpose flour

1 teaspoon paprika

1 teaspoon garlic powder

Salt

Freshly ground black pepper

Vegetable oil, for frying

4 tablespoons (½ stick, or 56 g) unsalted butter, melted

2 tablespoons (40 g) honey

2 sandwich buns, toasted

1. In a medium bowl, combine the chicken and buttermilk, turning to coat. Cover and refrigerate to marinate for at least 2 hours.

2. In another medium bowl, whisk the flour, paprika, garlic powder, and salt and pepper to taste to blend.

3. In a deep skillet over medium-high heat, heat 3 inches (7.5 cm) of oil until it reaches 350°F (177°C).

4. Remove the chicken from the marinade, dredge it in the flour mixture, and carefully add it to the hot oil. Fry for about 15 minutes, turning once, until golden brown and cooked through, with an internal temperature of 165°F (73°C).

5. In a small bowl, stir together the melted butter and honey. Brush the mixture on the toasted buns.

6. Place the fried chicken on the buns and serve.

KOWBIRD HOT SANDWICH

Yield: Serves 2 | Prep time: 10 minutes, plus at least 2 hours marinating time | Cook time: 15 minutes

A fiery idea was sparked at the genesis of Kowbird, among the eager crowds and wafting aromas of our pop-up beginnings. This sandwich wasn't just another item on the menu; it was a dare. Inspired by our journey from pop-up to permanent, this sandwich mirrors the heat and passion in every step. It's a sizzle that's more than spice; it's a tribute to strength and the burning desire to serve the extraordinary. It's our story—packed between buns and set aflame with passion.

---

2 (6-ounce, or 170 g) boneless, skinless chicken breasts, pounded thin

1 cup (240 ml) buttermilk

2 cups (248 g) all-purpose flour

1 tablespoon (5 g) cayenne pepper

1 teaspoon paprika

1 teaspoon garlic powder

Salt

Freshly ground black pepper

Vegetable oil, for frying

2 sandwich buns, toasted

Hot sauce, for drizzling

Shredded lettuce, for serving

Caramelized onions, for serving

Slice of cheese, for serving

Condiments of choice, for serving

1. In a medium bowl, combine the chicken and buttermilk, turning to coat. Cover and refrigerate to marinate for at least 2 hours.

2. In another medium bowl, whisk the flour, cayenne, paprika, garlic powder, and salt and black pepper to taste to blend.

3. In a deep skillet over medium-high heat, heat 3 inches (7.5 cm) of oil until it reaches 350°F (177°C).

4. Remove the chicken from the marinade, dredge it in the flour mixture, and carefully add it to the hot oil. Fry for about 15 minutes, turning once, until golden brown and cooked through, with an internal temperature of 165°F (73°C).

5. Serve the fried chicken on toasted buns, drizzled with hot sauce.

KOWBIRD CHICKEN
Smash Burger

Yield: Serves 4 | **Prep time: 10 minutes** | **Cook time: 10 minutes**

The Kowbird chicken smash burger stands unparalleled in the realm of culinary crossovers. This dish marries the irresistible charm of a classic smash burger with the soulful essence of chicken. Born from playful experimentation, it captures the spirit of pushing boundaries while staying rooted in tradition. As you sink your teeth into this fusion of flavors, let it enchant you with its good times and shared memories.

1 pound (454 g) ground chicken

1 teaspoon salt

½ teaspoon black pepper

½ teaspoon garlic powder

4 sandwich buns, toasted

Shredded lettuce, for serving

Sliced tomato, for serving

Condiments of choice,
 for serving

1. Place a large skillet over medium-high heat and let it heat.

2. Form the ground chicken into four patties. Season them all over with salt, pepper, and garlic powder.

3. Place the patties in the skillet and press down on them with a spatula to "smash" them. Cook for about 10 minutes, flipping halfway through, until fully done, with an internal temperature of 165°F (73°C).

4. Serve the burgers on toasted buns, topped with lettuce, tomato, and your favorite condiments.

4

SOUTHERN SIDES

SOUTHERN GREEN BEANS
with Bacon

Yield: Serves 4 to 6 | **Prep time: 10 minutes** | **Cook time: 12 minutes**

Infused with rich bacon flavor and cooked to tender perfection, these green beans are a welcome addition to Sunday meals—simple ingredients create a family favorite. The smoky bacon bits add a pop of saltiness to each bite. This dish is especially delicious if you are able to gather the beans from your garden.

4 bacon slices, chopped

1 onion, finely chopped

2 garlic cloves, minced

1 pound (454 g) green beans, trimmed

Salt

Freshly ground black pepper

1. In a large skillet over medium heat, cook the bacon for about 5 minutes until crispy. With a slotted spoon, transfer the bacon to a plate, leaving the bacon fat in the pan.

2. Add the onion and garlic to the skillet and sauté for about 3 minutes until translucent.

3. Add the green beans, season them with salt and pepper to taste, and cook for about 4 minutes until tender.

4. Stir in the bacon bits before serving.

5. Refrigerate leftovers in an airtight container for 3 to 5 days.

FRIED OKRA

Yield: Serves 4 to 6 | Prep time: 15 minutes | Cook time: 30 minutes

A true Southern delicacy, fried okra illustrates the Southern cook's ability to transform the simplest garden offerings into a golden, crispy delight. The light, crunchy breading gives way to tender, flavorful okra in a nostalgic journey to sun-soaked fields. This dish carries a story of summer afternoons spent with hands stained green from picking, and grandmothers teaching the art of the perfect fry.

1 pound (454 g) fresh okra, sliced

1 cup (240 ml) buttermilk

1 cup (140 g) cornmeal

1 teaspoon paprika

1 teaspoon garlic powder

Salt

Freshly ground black pepper

Vegetable oil, for frying

1. In a medium bowl, combine the okra and buttermilk and let soak in the refrigerator for at least 30 minutes.

2. In another medium bowl, whisk the cornmeal, paprika, garlic powder, and salt and pepper to taste to blend.

3. In a deep-fryer or medium skillet over medium-high heat, heat 2 inches (5 cm) of oil until it reaches 350°F (177°C).

4. Working in batches, remove the okra from the marinade, dredge it in the cornmeal batter, and carefully add it to the hot oil. Fry for 4 to 6 minutes until golden brown. Transfer to paper towels to drain. Repeat until all the okra is used.

HUSH PUPPIES

Yield: Serves 4 to 6 | Prep time: 10 minutes | Cook time: 8 minutes per batch

The memories of fish fries and riverside picnics come alive with each golden, crispy morsel of hush puppies. Crafted with a simple batter, hush puppies conjure communal feasts, laughter echoing over water, and the timeless charm of Southern hospitality.

1 cup (140 g) cornmeal

½ cup (62 g) all-purpose flour

1 teaspoon baking powder

½ teaspoon baking soda

½ teaspoon salt

1 onion, finely chopped

¾ cup (180 ml) buttermilk

1 large egg, beaten

Vegetable oil, for frying

1. In a medium bowl, stir together the cornmeal, flour, baking powder, baking soda, salt, and onion.
2. Stir in the buttermilk and egg to make a medium-thick batter.
3. In a deep-fryer or large skillet over medium-high heat, heat 2 inches (5 cm) of oil until it reaches 350°F (177°C).
4. Working in batches, carefully drop the batter by tablespoonfuls into the hot oil. Fry for about 8 minutes until the hush puppies are golden brown all over. Transfer to paper towels to drain.
5. Repeat until all the batter is used.

SWEET POTATO CASSEROLE
with Pecan Topping

Yield: Serves 4 to 6 | Prep time: 20 minutes | Cook time: 30 minutes

Southern soil seems to nurture perfectly sweet sweet potatoes, so recipes like this were a natural evolution. This casserole, with its velvety sweet potato base, embodies the golden hues of autumn. The crunchy pecan topping serves as a delectable testament to ingenuity in the kitchen.

For the sweet potato base

Nonstick cooking spray

3 cups (600 g) mashed, cooked sweet potatoes

½ cup (100 g) granulated sugar

½ cup (120 ml) milk

4 tablespoons (½ stick, or 56 g) unsalted butter, melted

2 large eggs, beaten

½ teaspoon vanilla extract

For the pecan topping

½ cup (120 g) packed brown sugar

¼ cup (31 g) all-purpose flour

4 tablespoons (½ stick, or 56 g) unsalted butter, melted

½ cup (55 g) chopped pecans

To make the sweet potato base

1. Preheat the oven to 375°F (190.5°C, or gas mark 5). Coat a 10-inch (25 cm) baking dish with cooking spray.

2. In a large bowl, stir together the sweet potatoes, granulated sugar, milk, butter, eggs, and vanilla until well combined. Transfer the mixture to the prepared baking dish. Set aside.

To make the pecan topping

3. In a medium bowl, stir together the brown sugar, flour, butter, and pecans. Sprinkle the topping over the sweet potato base.

4. Bake for 25 to 30 minutes, or until the topping is golden brown.

5. Cover and refrigerate leftovers for 3 to 5 days.

RED BEANS AND RICE

Yield: Serves 4 to 6 | Prep time: 15 minutes, plus overnight soaking time | Cook time: 3 hours

Every Monday—whether in the bayou or bustling streets of Louisiana's cities—a pot of simmering spices and beans turns Sunday's leftovers into Monday's feast. This humble dish, born from necessity, grew to symbolize the vibrant spirit of a region, uniting families around the dinner table. It reminds us that the simplest ingredients create the richest flavors and memories. Serve this with some home made corn bread (page 108).

---

1 pound (454 g) dried red beans, covered in water by 2 inches (5 cm) and soaked overnight

1 tablespoon (15 ml) olive oil

1 onion, chopped

2 celery stalks, chopped

1 bell pepper (any color), chopped

2 garlic cloves, minced

1 pound (454 g) andouille sausage, sliced

1 bay leaf

1 teaspoon chopped fresh thyme

Salt

Freshly ground black pepper

4 cups (740 g) cooked rice, still hot

1. Rinse and drain the beans.

2. In a large pot over medium heat, heat the oil until it shimmers. Add the onion, celery, bell pepper, and garlic and sauté for about 5 minutes until the onion is translucent.

3. Add the beans, sausage, bay leaf, and thyme. Season with salt and pepper to taste, then pour in enough water to cover the mixture by 2 inches (5 cm).

4. Bring the liquid to a boil, then reduce the heat to low and simmer for 2 to 3 hours, or until the beans are tender.

5. Serve the beans over the cooked rice.

6. Refrigerate leftovers in an airtight container for 3 to 5 days.

CHEESY GRITS

Yield: Serves 4 | **Prep time: 5 minutes** | **Cook time: 20 minutes**

Grits are the heart and soul of Southern comfort. Soft, creamy, and suffused with the warmth of molted cheese, each spoonful tells a tale of family breakfasts and laughter-filled brunches. It's a recipe passed down through generations, each adding its own touch, yet its essence remains unchanged: simple ingredients combined with love.

4 cups (960 ml) water

1 cup (140 g) grits

½ cup (60 g) grated Cheddar cheese

2 tablespoons (28 g) unsalted butter

Salt

Freshly ground black pepper

1. In a medium saucepan over medium-high heat, bring the water to a boil. Stir in the grits and reduce the heat to low. Cook for about 20 minutes until water is absorbed and the grits arc soft.

2. Stir in the cheese and butter until melted and well combined and season with salt and pepper to taste.

3. Refrigerate leftovers in an airtight container for 3 to 5 days.

MASHED POTATOES
with Garlic and Buttermilk

Yield: Serves 4 to 6 | **Prep time: 15 minutes** | **Cook time: 20 minutes**

Mashed potatoes bring me straight back to childhood. I can still feel the excitement bubbling whenever a whiff of that unmistakable aroma wafted through our home. I could've eaten them daily— I wouldn't have minded one bit. The creaminess of the potatoes, punctuated with the tang of buttermilk and the subtle bite of garlic, was pure comfort on a plate.

4 large potatoes, peeled and cut into 1-inch (2.5 cm) cubes

3 garlic cloves, minced

½ cup (120 ml) buttermilk

4 tablespoons (½ stick, or 56 g) butter

Salt

Freshly ground black pepper

1. Place the potatoes in a large saucepan and add enough water to cover them by 2 inches (5 cm). Place the pan over medium-high heat, bring the potatoes to a boil, then reduce the heat and simmer for about 20 minutes until they are tender. Drain the potatoes and return them to the pan.

2. Add the garlic, buttermilk, butter, and salt and pepper to taste. Mash the potatoes until smooth.

3. Refrigerate leftovers in an airtight container for 3 to 5 days.

FRIED GREEN TOMATOES
with Remoulade Sauce

Yield: Serves 4 | **Prep time: 15 minutes, plus 30 minutes soaking time** | **Cook time: 15 minutes**

As a child, I discovered this iconic preparation while impatiently waiting for tomatoes to ripen in the garden. Golden-crusted with the zesty kick of remoulade sauce, these tomatoes remind me of sun-drenched porches and cherished family get-togethers. Each slice carries the story of generations who knew how to turn the unripe into the unforgettable.

4 green tomatoes, sliced

1 cup (240 ml) buttermilk

1 cup (140 g) cornmeal

1 teaspoon paprika

1 teaspoon garlic powder

Salt

Freshly ground black pepper

Vegetable oil, for frying

½ recipe Remoulade Sauce (page 138)

1. In a medium bowl, combine the tomato slices and buttermilk and let soak in the refrigerator for at least 30 minutes.

2. In another medium bowl, whisk the cornmeal, paprika, garlic powder, and salt and pepper to taste until well combined.

3. In a deep-fryer or large skillet over medium-high heat, heat 2 inches (5 cm) of oil until it is shimmering.

4. Working in batches, remove the tomato slices from the marinade, dredge them in the cornmeal mixture, and carefully add them to the hot oil. Fry for about 3 minutes, turning once, until golden brown. Transfer to paper towels to drain. Repeat until all the slices are coated and fried.

5. Serve the fried green tomatoes with the remoulade sauce on the side.

My Family's
CORN BREAD

Yield: Serves 8 | Prep time: 15 minutes | Cook time: 25 minutes

There are dozens of spins on corn bread, and many claim to be "the" traditional Southern style. Some people like a denser and moister bread, whereas others want a drier and fluffier one. Some people want to taste the sweetness, others do not. This is the family corn bread recipe I grew up with, and it leans toward fluffy and sweet. The one thing on which everyone agrees? Cook your corn bread in a well-seasoned cast-iron pan.

8 tablespoons (1 stick, or 113 g) butter, melted, plus more for the baking dish

1½ cups (210 g) cornmeal

1½ cups (186 g) all-purpose flour

⅓ cup (67 g) sugar

1½ tablespoons (21 g) baking powder

1 to 1½ teaspoons salt

1½ cups (360 ml) milk

3 large eggs

¼ cup (80 g) honey

1. Preheat the oven to 400°F (204°C, or gas mark 6). Lightly coat a 9 × 13-inch (23 × 33 cm) baking dish with butter.

2. In a large bowl, whisk the cornmeal, flour, sugar, baking powder, and salt to blend.

3. In a small bowl, whisk the milk and eggs until blended. Add the milk mixture to the cornmeal mixture and stir until combined. Stir in the melted butter and honey. Pour the batter into the prepared baking dish.

4. Bake for about 25 minutes until the corn bread is lightly browned and a toothpick inserted into the center comes out clean.

CORN BREAD DRESSING

Yield: Serves 4 to 6 | Prep time: 10 minutes | Cook time: 50 minutes

*Steeped in Southern tradition, corn bread dressing is more than just a side dish;
each golden crumb carries the whispers of past generations—grandmothers and grandfathers who
lovingly prepared it for family feasts. Although the recipe has evolved, its essence remains unchanged—
gatherings, gratitude, and the timeless joy of sharing a meal.*

Nonstick cooking spray

4 cups (360 g) crumbled corn bread (such as My Family's Corn Bread, page 108)

2 cups (230 g) bread crumbs

1 onion, finely chopped

2 celery stalks, chopped

4 cups (960 ml) chicken broth

2 large eggs, beaten

1 teaspoon chopped fresh sage

Salt

Freshly ground black pepper

1. Preheat the oven to 375°F (190.5°C, or gas mark 5). Coat a 10-inch (25 cm) baking dish with cooking spray.

2. In a large bowl, combine the corn bread, bread crumbs, onion, and celery.

3. Add the broth, eggs, and sage. Season with salt and pepper to taste. Mix until the dressing is well combined. Transfer the dressing to the prepared baking dish.

4. Bake for 45 to 50 minutes, or until the dressing is set and golden brown.

5. If making ahead, or if there are leftovers, refrigerate the dressing in an airtight container for 3 to 5 days.

BIRD FRIES

Yield: Serves 4 to 6 | Prep time: 10 minutes | Cook time: 25 minutes

Bird fries are a playful blend of comfort and innovation at the heart of our culinary journey. They are a tribute to tradition and imagination, a tempting union of crispy fries, our zesty Southern Comeback Sauce, and deeply caramelized onions. Each bite is a delight, blending familiar comforts with bold, new twists.

3 large russet potatoes, cut into fries

2 tablespoons (30 ml) olive oil

1 teaspoon paprika

1 teaspoon garlic powder

1 teaspoon onion powder

Salt

Freshly ground black pepper

½ yellow onion, sliced thin

1 recipe Southern Comeback Sauce, page 136

1. Preheat the oven to 425°F (220°C, or gas mark 7).

2. In a medium bowl, toss the potatoes with the oil, paprika, garlic powder, onion powder, and salt and pepper to taste. Spread the fries on a baking sheet in a single layer.

3. Bake for 20 to 25 minutes, flipping halfway through, until crispy and golden.

4. Meanwhile, cook the onion slices in some oil over low heat in a skillet, turning them over once after 10 minutes, until they are caramelized, 18 to 20 minutes total. Very gently stir the onions together with the fries and serve with the Southern Comeback Sauce.

BISCUITS
with Honey Butter

Yield: Makes 12 biscuits | Prep time: 20 minutes | Cook time: 15 minutes

Biscuits hold a cherished spot in my treasured memories. Every flaky layer represents the many mornings I awoke to the gentle sound of a rolling pin and the smell of golden goodness baking. And the honey butter? It's liquid gold, sweet and velvety, a testament to nature's simplicity. Drizzling it over a warm biscuit was pure indulgence, making even the most ordinary mornings feel like a celebration.

For the honey butter

4 tablespoons (½ stick, or 56 g) butter, at room temperature

2 tablespoons (40 g) honey

For the biscuits

2 cups (248 g) all-purpose flour, plus more for dusting

1 tablespoon (14 g) baking powder

½ teaspoon salt

¼ teaspoon baking soda

6 tablespoons (¾ stick, or 84 g) cold unsalted butter, cubed

¾ cup (180 ml) buttermilk

To make the honey butter

1. In a small bowl, stir together the butter and honey until well blended. Set aside.

To make the biscuits

2. Preheat the oven to 450°F (230°C, or gas mark 8).

3. In a large bowl, whisk the flour, baking powder, salt, and baking soda until well combined. Using two forks or a pastry cutter, cut in the butter until the mixture resembles coarse crumbs.

4. Add the buttermilk and toss the mixture with a fork until just moistened.

5. Lightly dust a clean work surface with flour and turn the dough onto it. Knead the dough gently 8 to 10 times. Roll the dough to a 1-inch (2.5 cm) thickness. Using a floured 2-inch (5 cm) round cutter, cut out biscuits. Gather up the scraps, re-roll them, and cut out more biscuits. You should have about 12. Place the biscuits 2 inches (5 cm) apart on an ungreased baking sheet.

6. Bake the biscuits for 10 to 15 minutes, or until golden brown.

7. Serve the warm biscuits with the honey butter.

8. Store leftover biscuits in an airtight container at room temperature for up to 4 days.

5

DESSERTS

Classic
SOUTHERN PECAN PIE

Yield: Serves 8 | Prep time: 10 minutes | Cook time: 1 hour

My first delectable slice of this rich Southern tradition, with its golden sweet filling and toasted pecans, was enjoyed under a sprawling oak, and it came with stories describing the people who'd harvested pecans through the years. Let this recipe inspire your traditions.

1 unbaked 9-inch (23 cm) piecrust, store-bought or homemade

1 cup (200 g) sugar

1 cup (310 g) light corn syrup

4 large eggs

4 tablespoons (½ stick, or 56 g) unsalted butter, melted

1 teaspoon vanilla extract

1½ cups (150 g) coarsely chopped pecans

1. Preheat the oven to 350°F (177°C, or gas mark 4).

2. Fit the piecrust into a 9-inch (23 cm) pie pan and trim the edges, as needed.

3. In a large bowl, whisk the sugar, corn syrup, eggs, melted butter, and vanilla until smooth.

4. Stir in the chopped pecans and pour the filling into the piecrust.

5. Bake the pie for 50 minutes to 1 hour, or until the filling is set.

6. Let the pie cool on a wire rack before serving.

7. Cover and refrigerate leftovers for up to 5 days.

SWEET POTATO PIE

Yield: Serves 8 | Prep time: 10 minutes | Cook time: 1 hour

In the heart of Southern kitchens, sweet potato pie is a beacon of warmth and tradition. As a child, I watched in wonder as silky puréed sweet potatoes, fragrant spices, and a buttery crust transformed into something magical. Each slice is a comforting embrace, a story told, and a legacy passed from one kitchen to the next.

1 unbaked 9-inch (23 cm) piecrust, store-bought or homemade

2 cups (400 g) mashed cooked sweet potatoes

1 cup (200 g) sugar

½ cup (120 ml) evaporated milk

4 tablespoons (½ stick, or 56 g) unsalted butter, melted

2 large eggs

1 teaspoon vanilla extract

½ teaspoon ground cinnamon

¼ teaspoon ground nutmeg

1. Preheat the oven to 350°F (177°C, or gas mark 4).

2. Fit the piecrust into a 9-inch (23 cm) pie pan and trim the edges, as needed.

3. In a large bowl, whisk the sweet potatoes, sugar, evaporated milk, melted butter, eggs, vanilla, cinnamon, and nutmeg until smooth. Pour the mixture into the piecrust.

4. Bake the pie for 50 minutes to 1 hour, or until a knife inserted near the center of the pie comes out clean.

5. Let the pie cool on a wire rack before serving.

6. Cover and refrigerate leftovers for up to 5 days.

TIMELESS APPLE PIE

Yield: Serves 8 | Prep time: 20 minutes | Cook time: 50 minutes

Every crisp crust and spiced apple filling remind me of orchard trips, kitchen giggles, and the anticipation before that first warm bite. This apple pie recipe embodies family time and shared joys. Tuck into a slice, relive cherished celebrations, and craft new memories with each delicious bite.

6 cups (660 g) sliced, peeled apples (preferably Granny Smith)

1 tablespoon (15 ml) fresh lemon juice

¾ cup (150 g) granulated sugar

¼ cup (60 g) packed brown sugar

¼ cup (31 g) all-purpose flour, plus more for dusting

1½ teaspoons vanilla extract

1 teaspoon ground cinnamon

¼ teaspoon ground nutmeg

¼ teaspoon salt

2 unbaked 9-inch (23 cm) piecrusts, store-bought or homemade

2 tablespoons (28 g) unsalted butter, cut into small pieces

1. Preheat the oven to 425°F (220°C, or gas mark 7).

2. In a large bowl, toss together the apples and lemon juice. Add the granulated and brown sugars, flour, vanilla, cinnamon, nutmeg, and salt. Toss to coat the apples evenly.

3. Lightly dust a work surface with flour and roll out one piecrust on it to fit a 9-inch (23 cm) pie pan. Line the pan with the crust.

4. Fill the crust with the apple mixture and dot the apples with the butter.

5. Roll the second crust into a 10-inch (25 cm) round and place it over the apples. Crimp the edges of the crusts together to seal and cut slits in the top for steam to escape.

6. Bake the pie for 45 to 50 minutes, or until the crust is golden and the apples are tender. If the edges brown too quickly, cover them with aluminum foil.

7. Let the pie cool on a wire rack before serving.

8. Cover and refrigerate leftovers for up to 5 days.

BUTTERMILK PIE

Yield: Serves 8 | Prep time: 10 minutes | Cook time: 50 minutes

Buttermilk pie is a Southern gem, often overshadowed by its fancy pie counterparts but undoubtedly a star. Its creamy, tangy filling transports me back to my family's kitchen table, where stories flowed as freely as the buttermilk used in the pie. Experience this classic dessert's warmth, history, and sweetness, and let it work its magic into your family gatherings.

1 unbaked 9-inch (23 cm) piecrust, store-bought or homemade

1½ cups (300 g) sugar

8 tablespoons (1 stick, or 113 g) unsalted butter, melted

3 tablespoons (23 g) all-purpose flour

3 large eggs

1 cup (240 ml) buttermilk

1 teaspoon vanilla extract

1. Preheat the oven to 350°F (177°C, or gas mark 4).

2. Fit the piecrust into a 9-inch (23 cm) pie pan and trim the edges, as needed.

3. In a large bowl, whisk together the sugar, melted butter, and flour.

4. One at a time, beat in the eggs. Stir in the buttermilk and vanilla. Pour the mixture into the piecrust.

5. Bake the pie for 50 minutes, or until a knife inserted near the center of the pie comes out clean. The center may still be slightly jiggly.

6. Let the pie cool on a wire rack before serving.

7. Cover and refrigerate leftovers for up to 5 days.

BOURBON PECAN PIE

Yield: Serves 8 | Prep time: 10 minutes | Cook time: 1 hour

A heady blend of bold bourbon and crunchy pecans, this pie is reminiscent of warm nights on the porch, glasses clinking in celebration, and laughter echoing into the night. It's a melding of rich flavors and richer history—a pie best served with tall tales and a splash of bourbon on the side.

1 cup (200 g) sugar

¾ cup (232 g) light corn syrup

¼ cup (60 ml) bourbon

4 large eggs

4 tablespoons (½ stick, or 56 g) unsalted butter, melted

1 teaspoon vanilla extract

1½ cups (150 g) coarsely chopped pecans

1 unbaked 9-inch (23 cm) piecrust, store-bought or homemade

1. Preheat the oven to 350°F (177°C, or gas mark 4).
2. Fit the piecrust into a 9-inch (23 cm) pie pan and trim the edges, as needed.
3. In a large bowl, whisk the sugar, corn syrup, bourbon, eggs, melted butter, and vanilla until smooth.
4. Stir in the pecans and pour the filling into the piecrust.
5. Bake the pie for 50 minutes to 1 hour, or until the pie is set.
6. Let the pie cool on a wire rack before serving.
7. Cover and refrigerate leftovers for up to 5 days.

7UP CAKE

Yield: Serves 8 | Prep time: 10 minutes | Cook time: 1 hour and 15 minutes

With its zesty lemon-lime flavor and tender crumb, each bite of this dessert makes me smile remembering good times. Share a slice and let the effervescent taste of the South brighten your day.

Nonstick cooking spray

3 cups (372 g) all-purpose flour, plus more for dusting

1½ cups (3 sticks, or 339 g) unsalted butter, at room temperature

3 cups (600 g) sugar

5 large eggs

¾ cup (180 ml) 7Up soda

2 teaspoons lemon extract

1. Preheat the oven to 325°F (170°C, or gas mark 3). Coat a 10-inch (25 cm) Bundt pan with cooking spray and dust with flour, knocking out the excess. Set aside.

2. In a large bowl, using a handheld electric mixer, cream together the butter and sugar for about 5 minutes until light and fluffy.

3. One at a time, beat in the eggs, stopping to scrape down the sides of the bowl several times.

4. Mix in the flour, 7Up, and lemon extract until well combined. Pour the batter into the prepared Bundt pan.

5. Bake the cake for 1 hour to 1 hour and 15 minutes, or until a toothpick inserted into the center of the cake comes out clean.

6. Let the cake cool in the pan for about 20 minutes, then invert it onto a serving plate.

7. Cover and refrigerate leftovers for up to 5 days.

COCONUT CREAM PIE

Yield: Serves 8 | Prep time: 15 minutes, plus 2 hours chilling time | Cook time: 40 minutes

Coconut cream pie is a luscious ode to comfort, where silky custard meets the tropical allure of coconut. With each indulgent bite, I recall sultry summer evenings that melt into the sweetness of homemade desserts. This pie is an invitation to savor simplicity.

1 unbaked 9-inch (23 cm) piecrust, store-bought or homemade, chilled

1½ cups (120 g) sweetened flaked coconut

1 cup (200 g) sugar

¼ cup (32 g) cornstarch

½ teaspoon salt

3 cups (720 ml) milk

4 large egg yolks, beaten

1 tablespoon (14 g) unsalted butter

1 teaspoon vanilla extract

Whipped cream, for topping

1. Preheat the oven to 375°F (190.5°C, or gas mark 5).

2. Fit the piecrust into a 9-inch (23 cm) pie pan and trim the edges, as needed. Line the crust with parchment paper and fill it with pie weights or dried beans. Bake the crust for about 15 minutes until the edges start to set and brown.

3. Remove the crust from the oven and carefully lift the parchment and weights out of it. With a fork, prick holes all over the bottom of the crust and continue to bake for about 15 minutes more until the crust is golden brown.

4. While the crust bakes, place a skillet over medium heat and let it get hot. Add the coconut and toast, stirring, for about 2 minutes until browned to your liking. Transfer to a bowl to stop the cooking.

5. In a medium saucepan, whisk the sugar, cornstarch, and salt to blend. Gradually whisk in the milk. Place the pan over medium heat and cook for about 5 minutes, whisking constantly, until the mixture thickens and boils. Boil, whisking, for 2 minutes.

6. Place the egg yolks into a medium heatproof bowl and whisk half of the hot milk mixture into them. Add the yolk mixture into the hot mixture in the saucepan and whisk to incorporate. Boil, whisking, for 2 minutes.

7. Remove the saucepan from the heat. Stir in the butter, vanilla, and 1¼ cups (100 g) of coconut. Pour the filling into the baked piecrust, cover with plastic wrap, and chill for at least 2 hours.

8. Before serving, top the pie with whipped cream and sprinkle with the remaining coconut.

9. Cover and refrigerate leftovers for up to 5 days.

MISSISSIPPI MUD PIE

Yield: Serves 12 | Prep time: 10 minutes, plus 4 hours chilling time | Cook time: 1 minute

An irresistible blend of Southern flavors. Decadent layers of chocolate, gooey goodness, and a crumbly crust combine to create a dessert that's pure nostalgia. It's a slice of Mississippi life, and every bite is a reminder of Southern charm and good living.

1 (9.5-ounce, or 270 g) package chocolate sandwich cookies, crushed

8 tablespoons (1 stick, or 113 g) unsalted butter, melted

½ gallon (1.7 kg) chocolate ice cream, at room temperature

1 (16-ounce, or 454 g) jar hot fudge sauce

1 cup (110 g) chopped pecans

Whipped cream, for topping

1. In a medium bowl, stir together the crushed cookies and melted butter until well coated. Press the crumbs into the bottom of a 9 × 13-inch (23 × 33 cm) baking dish.

2. Spread the softened ice cream over the crust.

3. Warm the fudge sauce slightly in the microwave on high power, in 30-second increments, until it is pourable and spread it over the ice cream. Sprinkle with the pecans.

4. Freeze the pie for about 4 hours until firm.

5. Top with whipped cream to serve.

6. Cover and freeze leftovers for up to 5 days.

PEACH COBBLER

Yield: Serves 4 to 6 | Prep time: 15 minutes | Cook time: 1 hour

Peach cobbler is a love letter from the heart of the South, of Southern summers, where sun-drenched orchards produce ripe peaches that pair sweetly with buttery pastry. It's a taste of time, a reminder of lazy afternoons, and a sweet promise of comfort.

4 cups (680 g) sliced, peeled fresh peaches

1 cup (200 g) sugar, divided

1 teaspoon fresh lemon juice

½ teaspoon ground cinnamon

¼ teaspoon salt

1 cup (124 g) all-purpose flour

½ cup (120 ml) milk

1 teaspoon baking powder

8 tablespoons (1 stick, or 113 g) unsalted butter, melted

1. Preheat the oven to 325°F (170°C, or gas mark 3).

2. In a large bowl, gently stir together the peaches, ¾ cup (150 g) of sugar, lemon juice, cinnamon, and salt. Pour the mixture into a 9-inch (23 cm) square baking dish.

3. In a medium bowl, whisk the flour, milk, remaining ¼ cup (50 g) of sugar, and baking powder until smooth. Spread the batter evenly over the peaches.

4. Pour the melted butter over the batter.

5. Bake the cobbler for 50 minutes to 1 hour until the top is golden brown. Cool slightly before serving.

6. Cover and refrigerate leftovers for up to 5 days.

RED VELVET CAKE

Yield: Serves 4 to 6 | Prep time: 20 minutes | Cook time: 30 minutes

Red velvet cake, with its striking scarlet hue and velvety texture, is an invitation to savor the South's rich history and vibrant flavors. A touch of cocoa and luscious cream cheese frosting create a cake that celebrates Southern charm, where hospitality is as warm as the cake itself.

For the red velvet cake

Nonstick cooking spray

2½ cups (310 g) all-purpose flour, plus more for dusting

1½ cups (300 g) granulated sugar

1 teaspoon baking powder

1 teaspoon salt

1 teaspoon cocoa powder

1½ cups (360 ml) vegetable oil

1 cup (240 ml) buttermilk, at room temperature

2 large eggs

2 tablespoons (30 ml) red food coloring

1 teaspoon vanilla extract

1 teaspoon baking soda

1 teaspoon white vinegar

For the cream cheese frosting

1 pound (454 g) cream cheese, at room temperature

1 cup (2 sticks, or 226 g) unsalted butter, at room temperature

1 teaspoon vanilla extract

4 cups (448 g) sifted confectioners' sugar

To make the red velvet cake

1. Preheat the oven to 350°F (177°C, or gas mark 4). Coat two 9-inch (23 cm) cake pans with cooking spray and dust them with flour, knocking out the excess. Set aside.

2. In a medium bowl, sift together the flour, granulated sugar, baking powder, salt, and cocoa powder.

3. In a large bowl, using a handheld electric mixer, beat the oil, buttermilk, eggs, food coloring, and vanilla on medium speed until well combined.

4. Slowly add the dry ingredients to the wet ingredients and mix until smooth.

5. In a small bowl, combine the baking soda and vinegar and immediately fold the mixture into the batter. Divide the batter evenly between the prepared cake pans.

6. Bake for 25 to 30 minutes, or until a toothpick inserted into the center of the cakes comes out clean.

7. Let the cakes cool in the pans for 10 minutes, then transfer to a wire rack to cool completely.

To make the cream cheese frosting

8. In a large bowl, using a handheld electric mixer, beat the cream cheese, butter, and vanilla on medium speed until smooth.

9. Gradually add the confectioners' sugar and beat until creamy and lump-free.

10. Frost and stack the cooled cake layers.

11. Cover the cake and refrigerate for up to 5 days.

6

SOUTHERN SAUCES

Alabama
WHITE BARBECUE SAUCE

Yield: Makes 1½ cups (275 g) | Prep time: 10 minutes, plus 2 hours chilling time

Alabama white barbecue sauce is a creamy concoction that hails from the heart of Dixie, a tantalizing departure from the typical tomato-based sauce. Its bold blend of mayonnaise, vinegar, and spices highlights the art of flavor balance. Each brush of this sauce sings with the spirit of outdoor gatherings and backyard feasts, where tangy meets creamy in perfect harmony.

1 cup (225 g) mayonnaise

¼ cup (60 ml) white wine vinegar

1 tablespoon (9 g) coarsely ground black pepper

1 tablespoon (12.5 g) sugar

2 teaspoons prepared horseradish

1 teaspoon salt

1. In a medium bowl, whisk all the ingredients until smooth. Cover and refrigerate for at least 2 hours before serving to allow the flavors to meld.

2. Refrigerate the sauce in an airtight container for up to 1 week.

SOUTHERN COMEBACK SAUCE

Makes 1½ cups (375 g) | Prep time: 10 minutes, plus 1 hour chilling time

Southern comeback sauce is a journey into the heart of Southern cuisine, where every dip and drizzle carries a hint of nostalgia. This versatile sauce is a creamy, tangy, spicy blend. With each bite, I'm reminded of gatherings where fried delicacies met their perfect match and finger-licking tidbits reigned supreme.

1 cup (225 g) mayonnaise

¼ cup (60 g) ketchup

¼ cup (70 g) chili sauce

2 teaspoons Worcestershire sauce

1 teaspoon Dijon mustard

1 teaspoon onion powder

1 teaspoon garlic powder

½ teaspoon freshly ground black pepper

¼ teaspoon hot sauce

1. In a medium bowl, whisk all the ingredients until combined. Cover and refrigerate for at least 1 hour before serving to allow the flavors to meld.

2. Refrigerate the sauce in an airtight container for up to 1 week.

REMOULADE SAUCE

Yield: Makes 1¼ cups (300 g) | Prep time: 10 minutes, plus 1 hour chilling time

Remoulade sauce is a spirited celebration of bold taste. This classic condiment, with its creamy base and fiery undertones, embodies the essence of Louisiana's culinary heritage. It's a sauce that dances on the palate, a tango of zest, heat, and a touch of magic. Drizzle, dip, or spread it; remoulade sauce is a taste of Southern exuberance that elevates every dish it touches.

1 cup (225 g) mayonnaise

2 tablespoons (30 g) Dijon mustard

1 tablespoon (15 ml) fresh lemon juice

1 tablespoon (4 g) chopped fresh parsley

1 tablespoon (9 g) chopped capers

2 teaspoons hot sauce

2 teaspoons Worcestershire sauce

1 teaspoon paprika

2 garlic cloves, minced

Salt

Freshly ground black pepper

1. In a medium bowl, combine all the ingredients and whisk until well blended. Cover the sauce and refrigerate for at least 1 hour before serving to allow the flavors to meld.

2. Refrigerate the sauce in an airtight container for up to 1 week.

BUTTERMILK RANCH DRESSING

Yield: Makes 1¼ cups (360 g) | **Prep time: 10 minutes, plus 1 hour chilling time**

This beloved dressing is like a culinary hug. With its cool buttermilk base and herb-infused charm, each drop is a journey through the taste of the South, transforming ordinary greens into extraordinary bites and elevating vegetables to new—and delicious—levels.

½ cup (120 ml) buttermilk

½ cup (120 g) sour cream

¼ cup (115 g) mayonnaise

1 teaspoon fresh lemon juice

1 teaspoon dried dill weed

½ teaspoon dried parsley

½ teaspoon dried chives

1 garlic clove, minced

Salt

Freshly ground black pepper

1. In a small bowl, combine all the ingredients and whisk until smooth.

2. Taste and add salt and pepper, as needed. Cover and refrigerate the dressing for at least 1 hour before serving to allow the flavors to meld.

3. Refrigerate the dressing in an airtight container for up to 1 week.

7

GRAVIES FOR CHICKEN

Classic
SOUTHERN CHICKEN GRAVY

Yield: Makes 2 cups (480 ml) | Prep time: 5 minutes | Cook time: 5 minutes

Chicken gravy is central to Southern comfort food. This tempting gravy defines homemade goodness, where golden brown drippings and tender morsels of chicken create irresistible flavors. Pour it generously and let its warmth fill your heart and your plate.

3 tablespoons (42 g) unsalted butter

3 tablespoons (23 g) all-purpose flour

2 cups (480 ml) chicken broth or stock

Salt

Freshly ground black pepper

1. In a medium saucepan over medium heat, melt the butter.

2. Whisk in the flour and cook, whisking, for 1 to 2 minutes.

3. Gradually whisk in the broth and continue to cook for about 3 minutes, stirring, until the gravy thickens.

4. Taste and season with salt and pepper, as needed, and serve hot.

5. Refrigerate the gravy in an airtight container for up to 4 days.

COUNTRY SAUSAGE GRAVY

Yield: Makes 4 cups (960 ml) | Prep time: 5 minutes | Cook time: 10 minutes

Gravy gives food a warm and hearty embrace. This beloved staple whisks me away to cozy mornings and family gatherings. With its creamy texture and crumbled sausage, it tells the story of simple, delicious traditions. This gravy transforms buttery biscuits (see Biscuits with Honey Butter, page 113), or toast, into an iconic Southern dish, a taste of home in every ladleful.

1 pound (454 g) pork breakfast sausage

⅓ cup (41 g) all-purpose flour

3 cups (720 ml) whole milk

Salt

Freshly ground black pepper

1. In a large skillet over medium heat, cook the sausage for about 5 minutes, browning it and breaking it up into small pieces.

2. Sprinkle the flour over the browned sausage and cook, stirring, for 2 minutes.

3. Gradually whisk in the milk and bring the gravy to a simmer. Continue cooking and stirring for about 3 minutes until thickened.

4. Season with salt and pepper to taste and serve hot.

5. Refrigerate leftovers in an airtight container for up to 4 days.

TOMATO GRAVY
over Biscuits

Yield: Serves 4 to 6 | **Prep time: 10 minutes** | **Cook time: 12 minutes**

Tomato gravy is a Southern classic that sings with bright flavors. It's a gravy that warms the heart and the soul. This delightful recipe takes me back to lazy brunches, where the aroma of simmering tomatoes filled the air. Enjoy a plateful of these golden, gravy-drizzled biscuits, and delight in a simple taste of the South.

2 tablespoons (30 ml) bacon grease or (28 g) butter

¼ cup (40 g) finely chopped onion

2 tablespoons (15.5 g) all-purpose flour

2 cups (360 g) drained canned diced tomatoes

1 cup (240 ml) milk

Salt

Freshly ground black pepper

1 recipe prepared biscuits (see Biscuits with Honey Butter, page 113), warm

1. In a medium skillet over medium heat, heat the bacon grease until hot.

2. Add the onion and sauté for about 4 minutes until translucent.

3. Stir in the flour and cook, stirring, for 1 to 2 minutes.

4. Add the diced tomatoes and milk. Cook, stirring continuously, for about 5 minutes until the gravy thickens.

5. Taste and season with salt and pepper, as needed. Serve hot over the warm biscuits.

6. Refrigerate the gravy in an airtight container for up to 4 days. Store leftover biscuits in an airtight container at room temperature for up to 4 days.

Mama's
GIBLET GRAVY

Yield: Makes 4 cups (960 ml) | **Prep time: 10 minutes** | **Cook time: 1 hour and 10 minutes**

Giblet gravy is a cherished recipe born from the kitchen of my beloved mother—the undisputed queen of this Southern delicacy. Savor each ladleful of rich flavor and tender giblet pieces in a toast to her culinary legacy. Aside from chicken, this gravy also dresses up turkey and mashed potatoes.

Giblets from 1 turkey or chicken, about 1 to 1½ pounds

4 cups (960 ml) water

3 tablespoons (42 g) unsalted butter

3 tablespoons (23 g) all-purpose flour

Salt

Freshly ground black pepper

1. In a medium saucepan over medium-high heat, combine the giblets and water. Bring to a simmer, reduce the heat to low, and simmer for 1 hour. Drain the giblets, reserving the cooking liquid. Chop the giblets finely.

2. In another medium saucepan over medium-high heat, melt the butter. Add the flour and cook, whisking, for 1 to 2 minutes.

3. Slowly whisk in the reserved giblet cooking liquid.

4. Add the chopped giblets and cook, stirring constantly, for about 3 minutes until thickened.

5. Taste and season with salt and pepper, as needed, and serve hot.

6. Refrigerate the gravy in an airtight container for up to 4 days.

ONION GRAVY

Yield: Makes 2¼ cups (520 ml) | Prep time: 10 minutes | Cook time: 15 minutes

Onion gravy transforms the humble onion into a culinary star. Its rich, velvety texture and sweet, caramelized taste is a home-cooked tradition in my kitchen. This gravy makes every meal special.

3 tablespoons (42 g) unsalted butter

1 large onion, thinly sliced

3 tablespoons (23 g) all-purpose flour

2 cups (480 ml) beef broth or vegetable broth

Salt

Freshly ground black pepper

1. In a medium skillet over medium heat, melt the butter. Add the onion and sauté for about 7 minutes until caramelized.

2. Sprinkle in the flour and cook, stirring, for 2 minutes.

3. Gradually stir in the broth. Cook for about 3 minutes, stirring continuously, until the gravy thickens.

4. Taste and season the gravy with salt and pepper, as needed, and serve hot.

5. Refrigerate the gravy in an airtight container for up to 4 days.

RED-EYE GRAVY

Yield: Makes 1¾ cups (420 ml) | Prep time: 15 minutes | Cook time: 10 minutes

With its bold infusion of coffee, this spirited Southern staple is as captivating as it is comforting. With each pour, I relive hearty breakfasts with the aroma of coffee mingled with the scent of cured ham. Enjoy the richness of this gravy over ham or biscuits (or both) and experience a true Southern wake-up call.

¼ cup (60 ml) cooked ham drippings

1 cup (240 ml) black coffee

½ cup (120 ml) water

Salt

1. Pour the ham drippings into a medium skillet and place it over medium heat.

2. Slowly pour in the coffee and water and bring to a simmer. Cook for about 5 minutes, allowing the flavors to meld.

3. Taste and season the gravy with salt, as needed, and serve hot.

4. Refrigerate the gravy in an airtight container for up to 4 days.

BACON GRAVY

Yield: Makes 2½ cups (600 ml) | Prep time: 5 minutes | Cook time: 12 minutes

Bacon gravy is a mouthwatering ode to cozy kitchens and hearty tables, where the aroma of sizzling bacon fills the air. This rich delight is perfect for pouring generously over biscuits, or any dish, so that smoky bacon flavor can lift your meal to that next flavorful level.

6 bacon slices

3 tablespoons (45 ml) bacon grease

3 tablespoons (23 g) all-purpose flour

2 cups (480 ml) milk

Salt

Freshly ground black pepper

1. In a medium skillet over medium heat, cook the bacon for about 6 minutes, turning, until crisp. Using tongs, transfer the bacon to a plate, leaving the bacon fat in the pan.

2. Add the bacon grease to the skillet and let it melt.

3. Whisk in the flour and cook, whisking, for 2 minutes.

4. Gradually whisk in the milk and cook for about 3 minutes until the gravy thickens.

5. Crumble the cooked bacon into the gravy and stir to combine.

6. Taste and season the gravy with salt and pepper, as needed, and serve hot.

7. Refrigerate the gravy in an airtight container for up to 4 days.

MUSHROOM GRAVY

Yield: Makes 2¼ cups (520 ml) | Prep time: 10 minutes | Cook time: 10 minutes

Each spoonful of this velvety gravy is packed with mushrooms' deep, umami flavor. Let their earthy notes turn a simple meal into an extraordinary delight.

3 tablespoons (42 g) butter

1 cup (70 g) finely chopped mushrooms

3 tablespoons (23 g) all-purpose flour

2 cups (480 ml) beef broth or vegetable broth

Salt

Freshly ground black pepper

1. In a medium skillet over medium heat, melt the butter. Add the mushrooms and sauté for about 3 minutes until soft.

2. Add the flour and cook, whisking, for 2 minutes.

3. Gradually whisk in the broth. Cook for about 3 minutes, whisking continuously, until the gravy thickens.

4. Taste and season the gravy with salt and pepper, as needed, and serve hot.

5. Refrigerate the gravy in an airtight container for up to 4 days.

8

SEASONINGS FOR CHICKEN

CAJUN SEASONING

Yield: Makes 1¼ cups (127 g) | Prep time: 5 minutes

The two most popular Louisiana spice mixes for cooking chicken are called simply "Cajun seasoning" and "blackened seasoning." There are numerous recipes for each, and the two can overlap. Cajun seasoning tends to have more cayenne and be hotter, and to have more herbs.

5 tablespoons (35 g) paprika

3 tablespoons (30 g) salt

2 tablespoons (14 g) onion powder

2 tablespoons (18 g) garlic powder

2 tablespoons (6 g) dried oregano

2 tablespoons (4 g) dried basil

1 tablespoon (3 g) dried thyme

1 tablespoon (6 g) freshly ground black pepper

1 tablespoon (6 g) ground white pepper

1 tablespoon (5 g) cayenne pepper

1. In a small bowl, combine all the ingredients and mix them thoroughly.

2. Store in an airtight container at room temperature for up to 6 months.

CREOLE SEASONING

Yield: Makes scant 1 cup (90 g) | **Prep time: 5 minutes**

There are dozens of Creole seasoning mixes available in stores. Making the seasoning yourself saves a lot of money and allows you to tailor the blend to your taste. I keep this mix on hand at home for quick-fix chicken dinners and for all manner of fish and seafood.

3 tablespoons (21 g) paprika

2 tablespoons (14 g) onion powder

2 tablespoons (18 g) garlic powder

2 tablespoons (6 g) dried oregano

2 tablespoons (4 g) dried basil

1 tablespoon (3 g) dried thyme

1 tablespoon (9 g) freshly ground black pepper

1 tablespoon (5 g) cayenne pepper

1 tablespoon (10 g) salt

1. In a small bowl, combine all the ingredients and mix them thoroughly.
2. Store in an airtight container at room temperature for up to 6 months.

MEMPHIS DRY RUB

Yield: Makes 1¼ cups (173 g) | Prep time: 5 minutes

When you think of chicken from Tennessee, you think of Nashville Hot Chicken (page 52). Outside of Tennessee, Memphis is known for its smoked or grilled pork ribs. But, in reality, there are also amazing chicken dishes to be had all over Memphis, where the meat is typically rubbed before it is cooked—whether in the smoker or the oven, or on the grill or stovetop— with this classic sweet-and-hot Memphis seasoning.

¼ cup (28 g) paprika

¼ cup (60 g) packed brown sugar

3 tablespoons (27 g) freshly ground black pepper

2 tablespoons (18 g) garlic powder

2 tablespoons (14 g) onion powder

2 tablespoons (6 g) dried oregano

2 tablespoons (15 g) chili powder

1 tablespoon (5 g) cayenne pepper

1. In a small bowl, combine all the ingredients and mix them thoroughly.

2. Store in an airtight container at room temperature for up to 6 months.

LEMON PEPPER SEASONING

Yield: Makes heaping ¾ cup (106 g) | Prep time: 10 minutes

There's nothing fancy here. If you get your hands on some all-natural, free-range chicken and you want the natural flavor of the high-quality meat to shine through, this simple seasoning is a good choice. It adds a nice accent but doesn't compete with the bird.

Grated zest of 6 lemons (36 g), dried and finely ground

¼ cup (36 g) freshly ground black pepper

2 tablespoons (14 g) onion powder

2 tablespoons (20 g) salt

1. In a small bowl, combine all the ingredients and mix them thoroughly.

2. Store in an airtight container at room temperature for up to 6 months.

SOUTHERN BBQ RUB

Yield: Makes scant 1¼ cups (178 g) | Prep time: 5 minutes

"Sweet plus heat" is the underlying formula in a multitude of Southern barbecue rubs. This is a versatile everyday dry rub that delivers. I use it on everything from sheet pan thighs and drumsticks to any kind of chicken on the grill or in the smoker. Reduce the quantities of the chili powder and cayenne if your crew includes kids who do not like spicy food.

¼ cup (60 g) packed brown sugar

¼ cup (28 g) paprika

2 tablespoons (18 g) freshly ground black pepper

2 tablespoons (20 g) salt

2 tablespoons (15 g) chili powder

2 tablespoons (18 g) garlic powder

2 tablespoons (14 g) onion powder

1 tablespoon (5 g) cayenne pepper

1. In a small bowl, combine all the ingredients and mix them thoroughly.

2. Store in an airtight container at room temperature for up to 6 months.

BLACKENED SEASONING

Yield: Makes ½ cup (57 g) | Prep time: 5 minutes

Blackened dishes, among which blackened catfish is probably the best known, are made by heating dry spices in a skillet until very hot, adding a fish or meat to the skillet, then turning the fish or meat in the hot spices so a crust forms. As the food cooks to completion, the spice crust turns black, or nearly black, hence the name. It turns out that the Cajun recipe for such a spice mixture, which is now widely known as "blackened seasoning," offers a quick way to cook a Cajun-style piece of chicken, or whole bird, even if you are not using the dry-skillet method of blackening. Try it on oven-roasted or grilled chicken pieces.

2 tablespoons (14 g) paprika

1 tablespoon (5 g) cayenne pepper

1 tablespoon (7 g) onion powder

1 tablespoon (3 g) dried thyme

1 tablespoon (9 g) freshly ground black pepper

1 tablespoon (9 g) garlic powder

1 tablespoon (10 g) salt

1. In a small bowl, combine all the ingredients and mix them thoroughly.

2. Store in an airtight container at room temperature for up to 6 months.

A LOVE LETTER TO OAKLAND

Dear Oakland,

I write this from the depths of my soul, feeling every challenge, triumph, whisper of doubt, and shout of celebration that's been part of this culinary odyssey. Each step was unpredictable, with highs that touched the heavens and lows that tested my spirit. Yet, through it all, you, Oakland, stood tall and unyielding, a constant flame guiding me even in the darkest nights. Your streets, alive with history, have not merely narrated tales but also sung anthems of diverse cultures. These melodies found their way into my kitchen, crafting dishes as much a testament to you as they are to me. You welcomed this dreamer, not just with a nod but with an embrace, enabling me to feed bodies as well as nourish souls. Oakland, with your heartbeat echoing mine, I've found more than just my place—I've found my purpose. Here, amid your melodies and memories, I am more than a chef; I am a part of something larger, something timeless. Yet, no epic is complete without its storms.

To those who've stood in the shadows, casting doubts, aiming to dim the light of our collective dream, understand this: Every stone you throw and hurdle you place aren't just overcome. We take those stones and challenges and use them as a foundation, building monuments of resilience, passion, and unyielding spirit. Oakland, you're not just a geographical location but also a muse, an unending source of inspiration. Thank you for being the canvas upon which my dreams take shape and color. Thank you for reinforcing the belief that when food is stirred with love, dedication, and a touch of defiance, it becomes a universal anthem, transcending boundaries and connecting souls. Here's to the journey, the battles, and the unbreakable spirit.

With boundless love and gratitude,
Chef Matt Horn

"I am grateful for the hands woven into my story, leaving behind wisdom, love, and inspiration."

Acknowledgments

I am grateful for the hands woven into my story, leaving behind wisdom, love, and inspiration.

To my mentors, the culinary giants on whose shoulders I stand, who took a young, aspiring chef under their wings, nurturing my raw passion and molding it into art—I am because you were. You are the compass when I lost direction, the flame when my spirit waned, and the anchor in my most turbulent times.

Family is not just an institution but the very heartbeat of my existence. To my family, whose belief in me is unwavering even when I doubt myself, whose love is the warm embrace on cold, challenging nights, and whose faith lights the path when darkness threatens—my achievements are as much yours as they are mine. Your sacrifices, hopes, and dreams are the secret ingredients in every dish I create.

To the patrons of Kowbird, each of you is a cherished chapter in this delicious saga. When you walk into Kowbird, you do more than just dine; you celebrate a vision, trust a journey, and embrace a dream. It's one thing to create a dish, but another to see it resonate with souls, evoking memories, stirring emotions, and building connections. Every smile, every word of appreciation, and every constructive critique is the wind beneath my wings, urging me to soar higher and dream bigger.

Last, to the vibrant community that Kowbird has cultivated, thank you for being part of this voyage. You are not merely customers but co-travelers, sharing the joy of discovery, the intimacy of shared stories, and the universal language of food.

As I write these words, I realize that "thank you" is too small a phrase to encompass the ocean of gratitude I feel. Yet, from the deepest place in my heart, thank you. Here's to many more meals, memories, and milestones together.

With heartfelt gratitude,
Chef Matt Horn

About the Author

Matt Horn is the creator, chef, and owner of Kowbird in Oakland, California, a celebrated mecca for chicken lovers from the Bay Area and beyond. *Sunset* magazine has called Kowbird "a tribute to the South and the importance that chicken has played in African American culture," and Matt has told *Forbes* magazine that Kowbird "captures the essence of home and heart, influenced by my mother's touch." As the creative force behind AH2 Hospitality, Matt is also the chef/owner of Horn Barbecue in Oakland, which has earned Michelin Bib Gourmand and New Discovery designations and is where Matt's work led to his being named one of *Food & Wine* magazine's Best New Chefs in America; Matty's Old Fashioned, a diner, also in Oakland; and a second Kowbird location in Las Vegas. Matt and his restaurants have received hundreds of accolades from the *New York Times*, CBS Saturday Morning, *Sunset, Esquire, Forbes, Food & Wine, Robb Report*, and the *San Francisco Chronicle*, among other outlets. His charitable arm, the Horn Initiative, has provided thousands of free meals to those in need in and around Oakland. He lives with his wife, daughter, and son in the San Francisco Bay Area.

Index

Note: Page references in *italics* indicate photographs.